HOLISTIC PSYCHOLOGY OF ALEXANDER PINT

A MIRROR FOR THE PERSONALITY

INTRODUCTION FOR PRACTICAL SELF-INVESTIGATION

By ALEXANDER PINT

Translated by Emin Kuliev, MD

www.pint.ru

https://caterpillartobuterfly.wordpress.com

skyrocket press

Visit www.SkyrocketPress.com

Cover art by Freydoon Rassouli
ISBN: 978-1-944722-01-2

What does each one of us needs to meet himself? What do we need for self-investigation? We need to meet with a direct mirror that would show us who we are in reality. This book is about one of those meetings.

Thank you for your direct and indirect participation in the process of creation of this book.

TABLE OF CONTENTS

CHAPTER 1

SPIRITUAL EVOLUTION IS INTEGRATION OF THE OPPOSITES

· ◆·◆ · ◆·◆ · ◆·◆ · ◆·◆ · ◆·◆ · ◆·◆ · ◆·◆ · ◆·◆ · ◆·◆ · ◆·◆ · ◆·◆ · ◆·◆ ·

Who is moving and towards what?

— Let's get to know each other. Tell us how you got here and what your intention is.

— *My name is Oleg. I am an old member, and I have already said everything about my intentions. I've had many, and they were different.*

— And what's left?

— *A movement toward myself is the only thing that remains. How it will develop is difficult to guess.*

— A movement toward yourself remains. How about you? Are you here?

— *I am not sure.*

— So, the question is who is moving, and towards what?

— *I will see when I get there. Something is moving.*

— So, the one that is moving is not the one that one is moving toward? Then who is he?

— ...

— *My name is Violetta. I read your books, and I realized that I need to be here.*

— And why do you need to be here? You don't understand it yet?

— *I understand. There are quite a few questions, but in general, I want to understand myself better in order to better understand other human beings.*

— "To understand myself better in order to better understand other human beings." Good. And what do you find more important: to understand yourself or to understand other human beings?

— *I am not sure. I have to start somewhere. I think it's better to start with myself.*

— How does one understand other human beings?

— *One can only understand another through oneself.*

— **Are you saying we can only understand in another human being what we understand in ourselves? Do you mean we cannot understand in another man what we do not know in ourselves?** Is that right?

— *Well, another human being can teach us what we don't know or cannot do.*

— *The question here is what one's knowledge of oneself is.*

— You can come to college and professors will tell you what you do not know.

— *One can learn from his grandparents.*

— The question is what can one learn?

— *Perhaps one can open up something one did not even know existed inside him.*

— How can you open up something you do not know inside yourself? And how can you learn this from somebody else?

— *Perhaps we know it but hide it very well.*

2

— Okay. What do you hide about yourself?

— *I think...*

— *Kids remind us of something.*

— Kids remind us they want to have some candy.

— *Kids are different.*

— And what do your kids remind you of?

— *They remind me of who I am.*

— Are you a child?

— *No.*

— No?

— *They highlight the qualities of my character that I try not to think about.*

— And what do you try to think about when you don't think about these qualities?

— *I try to think that I am good, hospitable, and generous.*

— But kids show that you are bad, cheap, and greedy.

— *They can dig out stuff that one wants to hide.*

— And what are you?

— *I am different.*

— How?

— *Different.*

— So, you are good, but kids show you that you are bad. So, who are you?

— *I am both good and bad.*

— And how do you reconcile this?

— *When I don't accept what kids show me, I get irritable. Then I get angry.*

— So, being good and nice, you first get irritable, and then more and more angry?

— *Being nice sometimes...*

— Being nice sometimes? How about other times? How are you at other times?

3

— *We are all different.*

— I don't deny it. I am trying to figure out how we are, in reality. So, sometimes you are nice, and sometimes you are irritable and angry.

— *Yes, that happens. Why not?*

— I dont disagree. I am just asking.

— *When I start thinking about what my kid said to me, I sometimes see…deep inside…that is where the truth is.*

— So, what does your child points you toward?

— *Toward self-understanding.*

— In what way? "Self-understanding" is an abstract notion. What does it mean? That is why we gathered here. We want to figure this out. Please, next.

— *I am Sergei. I came because the internal is equal to the external, and certain things in the external world do not satisfy me.*

— Do you mean the external world does not satisfy you, but the internal does?

— *If those worlds are the same, then it does not matter how hard you push…I mean, situations change, but I am left alone. A man needs to start with himself.*

— So, the situations change, but you remain. The situations change, but you stay the same?

— *The result is the same. The first job, the second job, the third job—the result is the same.*

— So, the question is: "Does the situation change if the result is the same?"

— *Not really.*

— The situation does not change?

— *It does not.*

— We started with the fact that the external is equal to the internal. Then you said that the external changes, but the

4

internal remains the same. Now, we realize that the external also remains the same.

— *The point is that the internal does not change.*

— That's why the external does not change.

— *Well, yes.*

— So, does it change or not?

— *No.*

— And that brought up a thought that something needs to be done?

— *Correct.*

— Okay. Do you want to add anything?

— *We all evolve, life goes on, life evolves...*

— Life evolves, but what about you? We just figured out that nothing changes inside of you. Externally, as we realized, nothing changes either. So, nothing changes.

— *Time. We are limited by time.*

— Time flies.

— *Time flies, and I am interested in how to change myself. I am interested in the results. How can I achieve the results and change myself as fast as possible?*

— You want to act efficiently?

— *Yes.*

— And what does it mean to act efficiently?

— It means to receive what you want.

— And who is it? Who is the one that wants?

— The ego. Most likely it is the ego.

— And what happens to the desires of the ego? We just figured out that you have a desire to lead an efficient life. I asked a question: "Where is this desire coming from?" You answered: "From the ego." My next question: "Can the ego live efficiently?"

— *No. It cannot live efficiently.*

5

— How so? Economy should be efficient. People calculate and rationalize the optimum strategies in family life, children rearing, national development, etc. That is what happens here. But is it possible or not? That is the question.

— *Unlikely. I look at it differently. If you are on the right track, the economy will provide you with a result.*

— When does one start on the way toward an efficient life? Most likely one starts when one is born, and the end result is death. So, the strategy of an efficient life is to die more efficiently. Can we say so?

— *Well, if the goal is to die...*

— But all the goals at the end lead to death. The incident of our presence in this reality starts with the so called birth and ends with the so called death. Death is something no one can deny. Other things can be questioned, but not death. So, the only real goal of people that are born is death.

— *What kind of goal is it, if it comes on its own?*

— What do you mean, "It comes on its own"?

— *Well, if our time is limited?*

— But we want to live efficiently.

— *Interesting.*

— That's exactly what I offer—to get from birth to death more efficiently. Is not this the most important task from the point of view of efficiency?

— *I don't think so.*

— What do you mean? The only thing one definitely has is birth and death. Everything else is questionable. Every tomb has dates of birth and death on it, and a dash in between. Everything else is irrelevant. Those two dates are all that matters.

— *To whom do they matter?*

— For those who bury the dead.

— *Maybe for them. By the way, I am primarily interested in this dash in between.*

— Good. And when you are peacefully lying in your casket, would you be interested in the "by the way"? Another question: Why do people put those two dates and the dash in between on the tomb?

— *Does it mean their life was equivalent to zero?*

— I don't know. I am just asking a question.

— *Someone puts it. It is someone's judgment.*

— Strange people. Some of them later write: "To my dear father," "To the greatest lover from a loving lover," "To an amazing husband from a loving wife," "To an amazing worker from the coworkers." But those are addendums to the two main dates.

The spectacles of your perception

— *My name is Anton. I came here because I came here.*

— And I am sitting in a chair because I am sitting in a chair.

— *I was performing a stupid self-digging. It did not lead me anywhere. Then I discovered your books, and I understood that I do not know how to live in the "here and now." I wish I could. I cannot explain it in words. Certain changes occurred that led me here. I am grateful for that. I really enjoy being here.*

— Great. And what prevents you from living in the "here and now"?

— *One gets a desire to appraise oneself from the side. How do I look? I am afraid I would not measure up to somebody's expectations. There is a feeling of constraint.*

— And why don't we accept that there is a "here and now"?

7

— *Why don't we accept, or why don't I accept?*

— Why don't you accept?

— *Because I am stressed out.*

— And why are you stressed out? Look, acceptance or unacceptance of something comes from your perception.

— *Some kind of a block?*

— Each one of us has his own perception. You see many people around you. Each one has his or her own perception of a certain situation, in particular of what I say and what everyone around here says. Am I right? Everything is being determined by your perception.

— *It is like a smoke that clouds one's vision.*

— It is like a pair of glasses that we put on and then get identified with seeing through them, thinking that this is the only way. One says that it is hot in here, while another says that it is cold. The third one insists the temperature is normal. So, the situation is the same, but everyone's perception of it is different. Why do we perceive the same situation differently? How did we develop our perception?

It is our perception that does not allow us to accept what is here the way it is. For example, I smoke. Some of you do not like it, and you do not accept what is "here and now," in particular me and my smoking.

— *People have different beliefs.*

— Yes. Which one of you perceives that we should not smoke here? You and you. Excellent. You don't like the smoke. Therefore, you are not in the *here and now*, as you do not accept the situation as a whole. But this is only one of many fragments you do not accept. What other things don't you accept?

— *I did not expect you to smoke.*

— This is my present to you. You will get more presents in the future. If I were to stop smoking, you would experience other things you do not accept in me. For example, you may not like the color of my shirt or my glasses.

— *Come again. I missed it. If I were to remove my non-acceptance of one thing, my perception would still be partial?*

— Would you agree that you do not notice many things that are *here and now?* For example, what we hear with our ears is perceived in a very narrow diapason of frequency. Whatever is above or below this diapason, we do not perceive. Our physical vision works in a similarly narrow diapason.

Our physical vision sees only a very small diapason, but we think that we see everything. We also make conclusions regarding what exists, what does not exist, and what cannot exist. We happen to be in a dual world, and that makes everything even more interesting.

In the dual world there is good and there is bad, beautiful and ugly, smart and stupid. How does your brain relate to duality? Are you capable of seeing duality as it is? Can you perceive two opposite sides of duality simultaneously, or do you get fixated on only one of its sides? Five minutes ago, you said, "I am good." It means you do not accept yourself as being bad. Am I right?

— *I am different.*

— "I am different" is not a statement I can understand. What does "I am different" mean?

— *Sometimes I am this way, and sometimes I am that way. Life has many sides to it. How can one accept one side only? Today, let's say, you have this particular mood and those particular vibrations, and tomorrow when you feel completely different, you perceive different things.*

— Okay. How do you perceive your liver?

— *I am grateful to it for…*

9

— No. How do you perceive it? "Gratitude" is an attitude.

— *If it does not hurt, I do not notice it.*

— So, you do not notice it.

— *I don't.*

— Okay. How do you perceive your spleen?

— *The same way.*

— If it does not hurt, it does not exist?

— *It exists. If it did not exist, I would not be alive.*

— Theoretically you know it. And how do you know that you have a spleen? Do you believe the doctors who say you have a spleen, or do you perceive it inside yourself? And what kind of things do you have in you that you cannot see with physical vision?

— *After reading your books I know we have many other things.*

— The human body consists of millions of different cells. These cells unite to make organs that function. Complicated processes occur there. What do you know about those processes?

— *Nothing. I am sorry. We are not that smart.*

— What is it? A self-diagnosis?

— *We understand that we do not know much.*

— Are you saying you feel guilty in front of me because I asked you whether or not you see your spleen?

— *No, I don't feel guilty.*

— Well, you said, "Sorry." What was that about?

— *I did not pay attention to it.*

— In general, do you pay attention to what you say?

— *I am trying.*

— Are you trying or *do* you?

— *I am learning.*

— One can learn eternally. You said, "Sorry." That means you feel guilty. Or do you feel something else, when you say "Sorry"?

On what is not seen

— A human body is a microcosm, but a human being himself lives in a macrocosm. Now let's take one cell of a human body. A cell is a microcosm, and a microcosm is similar to a macrocosm. What kind of analogy to a macrocosm can you give me?

— *Solar system.*

— Exactly.

— *So, to a cell, a human being is a macrocosm.*

— Yes.

— *This is difficult because we don't know how it works. It is difficult to repair a refrigerator, but an appliance repairman has no problem doing it.*

— So, being a macrocosm, we do not understand it. I am showing you the limitations of our vision. Moreover, I can say that all the cells and organs of a human body are created by a certain collective consciousness, i.e. certain civilizations. Inside a human body different civilizations go through and acquire specific experiences.

— *We don't think about Jupiter. We don't think about our spleen and liver.*

— We don't think about anything except what we think about. We think in a certain way, and our thinking and perception of ourselves and the rest of the world is very limited. It can be compared to an ant's perception of a human being.

Do you think that the Earth contains only physical reality?

— *The Earth is a living being.*

— Yes. Earth is a living being. But does it contain only physical reality or is there something else?

— *Biosphere, noosphere, etc.*

— Okay, what else? And how about a human being: only a physical body or something else?

— *There are lots of other things.*

— Where do thoughts come from? Where do feelings come from?

— *Thoughts come and they go.*

— Everything comes and goes, but where do they come from and where do they go?

— *I think every single human being attracts certain thoughts.*

— Where do they come from? Can we physically touch them? We can embody a thought into something physical, but we cannot touch it. So, where does a thought live?

— *There is different energy there, different fields.*

— A thought inhabits different vibrational fields, fields that have higher frequency of vibrations than the material objects.

— *Are all of them superimposed on each other, or are they separate?*

— Aside from the visible physical objects, there are also astral objects—feelings, mental objects, thoughts, and many other things that are difficult to think about using our conditioned mind. A human being cannot be defined by physical form alone. So, where do feelings and thoughts come from?

— *Well, a liver lives in the physical body, thoughts live in the mental body, and feelings live in the emotional body.*

— *Feelings can be felt, but thoughts cannot be felt.*

— Interesting. You say that you are here to learn, but you behave as a teacher. We just learned that you do not know everything that well, at least in regards to your spleen. However, you talk about something else quite assuredly. You explain things to us. I, on the other hand, only ask questions. I cannot even say that I explain anything. I just ask the questions. But you explain things.

— *I am sorry.*

— Apologies again. What do you feel when you say this wonderful word "sorry?"

— *I feel irritation.*

— **Okay. You feel irritated, but it is not appropriate to express irritation for a polite and intelligent human being. Therefore, you substitute it by the opposite feeling—the feeling of guilt.**

— *No.*

— No?

— *I don't feel guilty.*

— Then why do you apologize so many times?

— *That is the accepted society way.*

— In what society?

— *In a collective society.*

— In what collective society: socialist, communist, or capitalist?

— *The last day of the seminar will tell us what kind of a society.*

— Now you are blaming. You feel irritated and you express aggression. You want to blame me for something, but you think that blame is not supposed to be manifested in the so called polite society. So, it is more appropriate for you to show your guilt, even though you feel blame right now. You do not express this blame, but you use words that point to the presence of guilt in you. And you say that you do not feel this guilt.

— *Why? I noticed that you smoke.*

— Okay. You noticed that I smoke, but you did not notice yourself covering up blame by guilt. Moreover, you don't even want to acknowledge it.

— *Are those two the only possibilities?*

— Yes.

— So, if I want to put blame on someone, but don't do it, I artificially create a feeling of guilt inside myself.

— Yes. Every game played in this reality on the level of vibration that the majority of people happen to occupy can be seen as a "Victim—Oppressor" game. The feelings that players experience in this game are blame and guilt. The oppressor blames a victim, and victim experiences guilt. But the victim is simultaneously the oppressor, because it is the victim who stimulates the so called oppressor to blame. This reality is dual. It is dual in the perception of the conditioned mind and the false personality people believe themselves to be.

Our process is a process of exiting three dimensional reality. This is only possible through the expansion of consciousness, through an increase of its vibrations. The consciousness of a human being is not limited by the diapason of the vibrations he is currently used to, being identifying with the conditioned mind and the false personality.

The opportunity of so called spiritual growth, in my opinion, is the opportunity to exit the limits of duality, the limits of our conditioning. You can already see the resistance of your conditioned mind. It happens because the questions I ask cannot be easily fitted into its habitual, one-sided mode of thinking. I am going to constantly stimulate you to see this conditionality. I call it awareness.

14

Your notions of yourself are real illusions

— Awareness is an opportunity to change the level of the vibration of consciousness that is limited by dual perception. It's an opportunity to see yourself the way you are now. It allows you to obtain practical results. Everything else is just staggering through the illusions. These illusions can be pretty, not so pretty, smart, and not so smart, but these are the illusions.

Becoming aware of your illusory notions about yourself provides an opportunity of experiencing yourself as a Human Being. You may not understand some of the things I say now, but this is a necessary condition for our moving forward.

Your first step on this journey is to see that your notions about yourself are illusory. Your views of the world are also illusory. Our process investigates the illusions, and allows us to see them as such.

— *One may have an idea of what an "illusion" is. Can one feel what an illusion is?*

— This is a new group, and I start from scratch. I can tell you how everything is, but it is going to be a lecture. I am not giving lectures, as they do not help practically. We take part in self-investigation.

Self-investigation is not a simple process, and it is practically unknown in this reality. It is unknown because the majority of people happen to be totally identified with the illusory, dual notions this reality is built upon. Next, please.

— *My name is Reda. I don't have a clear intent on being here, but I expect to figure it out in the process. The fact that I am here means that it is as it should be.*

— Look, this is a paradox. You do not have a clear intent to be here, but you are present here. **A paradox is a superposition of two contradictory tendencies. It is a duality. We can call it duality, or we can use the term paradox.**

The thinking process of a human being is fragmented. It only fixates on one aspect of a duality. In this particular case, Reda says, "I do not have the intention to be here." But she is here. It means that on a conscious level she notices something that she does not feel or see. She does not know the intent that brought her here, but she is here. She does not understand why. She is not aware of it. This is the perception of people conditioned by the convictions of the dual mind that we are going to explore and become aware of during our investigation.

One of the peculiarities of single-sided, fragmented thinking is the presence of blame and guilt. Our personality is an illusory structure that consists of two opposite halves. We are constantly dealing with a very interesting situation, when one side of our personality constantly blames another, opposite side.

For example, you consider yourself to be a good man. What exactly this means needs to be figured out, as "good" is a generic term. At the same time you also have a personal side which is bad. So, consciously you notice only one part of your personality—the part that you call "good." The part you call bad, you do not see in yourself, even though you act out of it all the time.

— *We have seen it.*

— No, you have not seen it yet. Currently, we are just probing your conscious and subconscious contents. The most important question every one of you should ask is, "Do I know that practically all my knowledge of myself is illusory?" When you start to feel that you do not know who you really are, you will make the first step in the direction of movement of our process.

If you do not even allow an assumption that you know practically nothing about yourself to enter your consciousness, you will resist everything that does not correspond to the conditioned notions of your mind. You will feel irritation and dissatisfaction, which will turn into hatred and aggression toward me and everything I say.

On the other hand, you can start to suppress your negativity, considering it to be inappropriate to express in public. In such case you will feel guilty—"I don't understand something." You will see this fluctuation between guilt and blame all the time.

The one who blames says his "truth" and blames another for not seeing it. But another one has his own "truth." This is the game people occupy themselves with. They blame other people who have opposite truths. Those other people blame them in return.

Our life is the unity of the oppositions

— I am introducing you to the ABC of self-investigation. A human being the way he currently exists is represented by the false personality that consists of two opposite parts. It is similar to two competing directors directing one show. Life is a show. Your life is your show. How do you create your show?

It is created by these two directors. One of them is being allowed to the level of consciousness, i.e. you are aware of what he creates, and you can tell us about it. The other director is subconscious. He also directs and creates

17

constantly, but your conscious part does not know what the subconscious part is doing. And what this part is doing is completely opposite to what the conscious part is doing. This is how duality, inherent to this reality and fixated in the perception of every human being, is realized. It is very important for us to understand the concept of the dual perception in which we are currently submerged.

— *So, when I blame myself, I simultaneously blame another human being for the same thing, right?*

— Correct. I blame others for something I do not accept in myself. I get into the role of an oppressor in relationship to them. I tell them, "This is not right. You cannot do this." I blame them, but the reason I blame them is that I project onto them what I do not see in myself. I cannot accept another human being until I accept what I blame him for in myself.

— How can one accept someone?

— This is a sly topic. Some say, "Let's accept everyone. Let's love everyone." Those are the slogans that are used by many people, but from the point of view of duality, you cannot accept another human being until you have accepted in yourself what you do not accept in him or her. Otherwise, it is simply impossible. So, what don't you accept in yourself? That is the main question.

The majority of people think that they know the truth. At the same time, another side of this truth, i.e. not-truth or a lie, is being assigned to other people, people they blame and fight with. One can get an impression that deceit is a characteristic of other people only. This is the major illusion of the dividing thought process and dividing perception.

What occurs in this reality is not real in the sense that it does not really exist. Everything that exists here is born out of mental activity of the conditioned mind that has a very

18

interesting peculiarity: everything it does with its right hand, it immediately breaks with its left hand. For every single desire that appears in a human being there is a contrary desire.

This is how the false personality is built. It has both positive and negative tendencies. However, because man is not fully aware of himself, he says, "Let's be positive. Let's not be negative." Then he starts a crusade against the negative in the outside world. That is what most of the people are doing using religious, economical, or political grounds.

— *Is it possible to simultaneously have a desire, to be aware of this desire, and to move forward with it, to act?*

— I want to specify the difference between what I call a desire and what I call intent. **Intent comes from the part of you that is not dual, i.e. from the Soul. A desire comes from a part of you that is dual, from your personality**.

The personality is dual. It has two opposite sides. I repeat, for every desire of yours, there is an opposite desire. That explains so called here mistakes, misfortunes, and catastrophes that occur.

What brings them on? The majority of people, having dual perception, see themselves separated from everything and everyone else. When something opposite to what they consciously want happens to them, they blame others for it. They feel someone fooled them or that they committed a mistake.

People invent different explanations to justify why what was not supposed to happen happened, completely oblivious to the fact that they have created it on their own. This is a consequence of the fact that a human being is not aware of himself. One sees himself as being whole and undivided, while in reality one consists of a personality comprised of many dual parts.

19

Only when the holistic level of consciousness is reached, will you understand that you are completely responsible for what is happening in your life. If you are saying, "I am a creator, I am whole," you should understand that **everything** that happens in your life is created by you and only by you. Then how can we explain the fact that certain things appear in your life that do not correspond to what you desire and expect? For example, you wanted to be rich, but you are losing money. You want to be healthy, but suddenly you get sick.

— *This is manifestation of the opposite side.*

— Yes. You wanted to be happy, but you are miserable. You wanted to be strong, but you turned out to be weak. Does it happen?

— *It seems we don't know what we create.*

— *So, if I desire something, I should also think about what I do not desire. I am responsible for it.*

Two directors: positive and negative

— You cannot remember it because the fragmented mind is built in such a way that it erases from our memory everything related to the activity of the director of, let's say, a negative character. We can say that you have the positive director and the negative director.

The majority of people are ready to accept responsibility for what they create consciously. Let's call it the creation of the positive director. But in the life of every human being, certain situations occur constantly that are being perceived by one as negative. Who and what are these negative situations related to? Why do they happen in your life? People try to fight it, but to no avail. Religion introduced the devil to explain the negative.

— *We don't see it.*

— We don't see it, and we don't remember it, because one half of our personality is in subconsciousness and creates surreptitiously. The conscious part of the personality that one considers to be himself does not allow one to accept the responsibility for thoughts, feelings, and actions that are related to its subconscious half. The conscious half of the personality tries to push away and to erase the memory of the subconscious part.

If you were to recall your life show, you would most likely see only one half of it. It is as if while listening to music you were only to perceive the major, and not to perceive the minor at all. To use a different analogy, it is similar to watching a movie that is interrupted every five minutes and to be resumed no one knows when. No one can understand anything.

But that is precisely how the memory of a human being is made. That is why one does not remember the major portion of one's own life. This will continue until you start to perceive yourself as a whole, as positive and negative simultaneously. This holistic acceptance of yourself is only possible on the next, higher frequency level of consciousness. Our process represents a movement toward this quality of consciousness.

— *The next step will make us understand that everything happens because it just happens.*

— **You need to figure out how you create what you create in your life. Everything that happens in your life is your creation.**

— *I create the appearance that I do something. The result of my actions is this good or bad that I perceive as good or as bad.*

— How do you know that good is good, and that bad is bad?

— *Life experience.*

21

— What is life experience? How do you know, for example, that this water is hot?

— *I don't know. I can try and prove it.*

— How would you prove it? Based on what would you make a conclusion that it is hot?

— *I would touch it with my hand.*

— Okay. You touched it. Then what?

— *I can become aware of the temperature: hot or cold.*

— How would you become aware of water being hot or cold?

— *By comparing it to something else.*

— The mind works based on comparison. If there is no comparison, the mind would not be able to appraise and to come up with judgment, to execute its main function. So, in order for you to know what goodness is, you need to know what evil is. Positive and negative are just two sides of one coin.

— *To be honest, I don't understand what good is and what evil is.*

— Let's say you consider yourself to be good. What do you base such a conclusion on? You need the opposite with which to compare. Otherwise, you will not be able to come up with a judgment. This is related to any personal quality. Every single one of us here has certain personal characteristics that his or her self-identification is based upon.

How do you become conscious of yourself? Who are you?

— *I have read…*

— And if you did not read, you would not know who you are?

— *No, I would not.*

— And how do you live like this, not knowing who you are?

— Well, I have a first name and a last name.

— Okay, so you think you are the first name and the last name.

— *There are certain convictions I live my life based upon. Education. Upbringing. That is what brought me here. I wanted to know who I am and why some things that happened to me prior to today do not satisfy me. Why am I so unhappy? Why does all of this lead me to physical death, precisely physical death? That's what brought me here.*

— Prior to reading my book, you lived and you had a certain notion about yourself. You would not be able to live; you would not even be able to get out of bed if you did not have a certain notion of yourself. You have one. So, I am asking you, "What is it?"

— *I thought that I was a separate being, which, similarly to a cocoon or a hard nutshell, had to defend my opinions and convictions.*

— Okay. A policeman approaches you asking, "Who are you?" You answer, "I am a being in a separate cocoon. I am defending my convictions, and my convictions tell me that you, the essence in a police uniform, should get away from me." What will he do? He will bring a couple of other essences dressed in police uniforms and take you to jail. What do they need from you?

— *My identification card.*

— And what is written there?

— *My name.*

— Perhaps you are just a name. We are just exploring the notion you have about yourself. The policeman does not need to know that you are a multidimensional being with twelve

23

chakras. He needs your passport, and until this passport is shown, whatever you say will just aggravate him.

— And not only him.

— Yes, not only him, because there are certain notions, quite widespread here, and what we call life here follows these notions. So, who are you? What kind of notions of yourself do you live with?

— *I live with contradictory notions.*

— You are not a spring chicken. How do you live? Based on what?

— *Based on other people's opinion of me.*

— But you probably have some notions about yourself? You must have been upset, angry, nervous, and resentful. Have you experienced these feelings? If someone comes to you saying, "You are such a great guy, I love you so much," you start feeling pleasure. But if someone says, "You are a stupid son of a bitch. I am going to hit you with a hammer," you experience irritation. Is that so? But why don't you say, "Yes, I am a stupid son of a bitch. Please, hit me with a hammer." He hits you, and you rejoice. Can something like this happen?

— *Yes, this can happen.*

— So, are you a stupid son of a bitch or a great guy? Who are you? And why do you react differently to what people do?

— *When the qualities of my personality are praised, I feel good.*

— So, you do rejoice when other people praise you for what you consider to be good?

— *Yes.*

— Okay. Who can say something in regards to what makes him or her happy?

— *I will feel happy when all my teeth are filled and I am not in pain.*

— But teeth are there not just to hurt. You use them for eating. Perhaps, you have difficult time eating? Teeth also represent one of the attributes of your physical appearance. If your teeth are bad, people may see you as ugly. Is that important to you? Imagine that you are toothless, for example.

— *It is uncomfortable.*

— So, for you it is not so important whether or not you are handsome, but to be comfortable during meals is important. For someone else, being handsome or ugly might be more important. Are there people here who would attest to that?

— *This is one of many reasons one may desire to have good teeth.*

— There are many reasons, and everyones' reasons are different. If I think I should be pretty and consider myself pretty, I would go to a dentist, not because my teeth hurt when I try to chew, but because I am not pretty now. I need to become pretty. When my teeth are done, I will feel better because I am pretty. Another person may not give a damn whether he is pretty or not; he finds it important not to be in pain. Is that so?

— *Yes.*

— So, every one of us has certain notions about himself or herself. When others confirm our notions about ourselves, we experience pleasure. When others deny our notions about ourselves, we experience displeasure. The degree of feeling pleasure and displeasure is different, starting from irritation and ending with hysterics and anger. **A human being can be easily brought to hysterics if he is constantly told that he does not correspond to his notions of himself.**

So, let's figure out what kind of notions of yourself you react to with irritation. Let's pair up and work on it. To what

25

kind of statements about yourself do you react with irritation? Which statements are really horrible for you?

Who is ready to state the qualities he denies in himself? If someone tells you about them, you get irritable, hateful, and angry.

— *I feel irritation when someone tells me what to do. I got to the duality "perfection—imperfection." My ideal vision of myself as being perfect cannot tolerate another point of view, because I think I am perfect.*

— It may also be other dualities: "dependence— independence" or "employer—employee." You mention one duality, and I show you that many other dualities exist. You will need to see them in your personality. You are the only one who can see them. Nobody else can do it for you. I only create the opportunity for this work. Actually, our group creates these unique opportunities. If you feel it, you will use these opportunities. These opportunities allow you to lead self-investigation.

The aim of self-investigation at this step is to detect and to become aware of the dualities present in your personality. Your fate or life-show you play within this physical reality is determined by the dualities present in your personality.

You are talking now about a certain duality that is important for you now. It means that it is being actualized by you. You perceive this show from the point of view of this particular, and possibly few others, present in your personality, dualities. It is precisely the activation of the dualities by your personality that determines the character of your life.

For example, if I consider myself free, then any action of other people forcing me to do something is perceived by me as slavery. These actions will cause me to experience negative emotions. "I am free. Nobody should force me to do what I do not want to do." But they do force me to do something, and I am unhappy. This situation points to the duality that is activated in you. In the process of self-investigation you will go deeper. You will see and specify the dualities present in your personality. That will give you a start in seeing how your fate is created.

Start to wake up. It is extremely important.

— How do you create your life? Why do certain events take place? Why do certain thoughts or feelings appear? Why do certain people get attracted to you? Why do they do what they do? By posing these questions and answering them, you can start to see why you live the way you live. When you start to see it, you start to see who you are at the present time.

You start to see that you can change your notions of yourself and, as a result, have different experiences. The result of a spiritual development can be viewed as a level of self-awareness one can achieve. The highest level of awareness of yourself that you can hold is your highest achievement at a given time. But self-understanding is limitless.

We start with level one. Essentially, a human being the way he is now is analogous to a new born baby. What does such a baby do? He sleeps most of the time. He eats and almost immediately falls asleep. He dreams.

A human being, the way he is now, is similar to this baby. He is asleep. What he considers to be reality is his dream. Our process is a challenge to wake up. To start to wake up means to start to see the dream one is dreaming, considering it to be one's life. If this is a dream, I can change it. Right?

27

— The question is how?

— This question will constantly appear in your mind. The mind does not even hear this discussion, but it constantly asks, "How? How? How?" Are you saying I can become a creator? How? Are you saying I can become an intergalactic creator? How? One should drink a glass of orange juice before bedtime, get up two hours later, prepare some soup from the old shoe, get to the roof, and eat the whole pot. If you don't vomit afterwards, you can become a creator. You want more?

I am introducing you to the concept of self-investigation. By getting a taste of it, you would better understand your questions. By understanding your questions, you would receive your own answers from inside of you. For now, the most important thing for you is to become aware of the dualities that are being activated by your personality. Different people have different combinations of dualities that comprise their personalities, but the principals governing the buildup of personal structures of people are the same. Those are the principals I am discussing now.

All personalities are as different as snowflakes, but the one who understands the mechanism of creation of a snowflake can discuss their variations. I am showing you how this reality, the conditioned mind and the false personality, operate. You can prove this by conducting your own self-investigation. Your life scenario is different from the scenario of other people. It is individual. However, the mechanisms that realize this scenario are identical for everyone.

People say, "One is not born with a personality; one becomes a personality." We have many personalities gathered here. What is a personality? What is your personality? It is a compilation of certain qualities. For example, kind—mean, handsome—ugly, smart—stupid. Those are qualities.

— It is a characteristic.

— It is a quality. You can use the word characteristic. Your mind is going to experience quite a difficult state now, because I offer you some new terms and give them a certain meaning. You may have encountered the terms I use, but you may have understood them completely differently. Now you would need to understand the meanings I give them. It is not easy, because one word can be used to express different notions. For example, "I love you." What does it mean? Someone says, "I love you," assuming that another understands it exactly the same way he understands it.

— Then why does he say it?

— He is a small child that is asleep. He dreams different dreams in which he talks, not understanding what he is talking about. But our task is to awake, and we need to learn to understand what we are saying, i.e. we need to become aware of ourselves. The first thing I want to emphasize is that a human being does not understand what he says. One uses certain words, but does not understand what they really mean. One does not understand because one does not know who he really is.

— Should one know who he is?

— Well, that is why we gathered here. A human being through the course of the day constantly uses the word "I," — I want this, I want that, I am insulted, etc.— without any awareness of who he is. This is a paradox. You do not understand who you are, but nevertheless, you constantly use the word "I" as if you did.

We are solving one of the most important puzzles, and it is very important to understand that, in reality, you do not understand yourself. You do not know that you do not know yourself. You think that you know yourself, but you do not

29

know yourself. At the same time, you have many illusory notions in regards to who you are. It is precisely these notions that create an illusion that you know yourself.

In addition, you also have the unconscious notions of yourself, according to which you act. Life in a state of sleep is training, and we are trying to figure out how it is organized. I am telling you that this training is based on duality. Our personality participates in this training. What do you think it is that becomes a personality?

— *A human being forms certain personal qualities.*

— Why does a given personality acquire specifically those and not some other qualities? They are different in every human being. Why did you acquire this particular structure of personality and not a different structure?

— *Parental upbringing. Parents inculcated these qualities into us.*

— Then why were you born to these particular parents who inculcated these specific qualities into you? Yes, your parents did it, but why were you born to these particular parents?

— *Most likely the Supreme "I" arranged that, so one would live through certain experiences and learn to be aware.*

— Okay, we provisionally can call ourselves Supreme "I," even though at the present time we do not have a full understanding of what it is. In the process of self-investigation we will understand this better. So, the Supreme "I" sends a certain projection here, which then, through a certain structure of qualities attributed to it, forms into a personality that determines its life.

For example, why are not you at war right now? There are always multiple "hot spots" on the planet. You did not go to war, you came to the seminar.

— *I want to live.*

— If you were to ask a soldier who is at war now to answer this question, he would say the same thing. Soldiers also want to live. They want to survive. They need to survive. The true soldier is the one who survives in the most difficult conditions. And why are not you in a whorehouse but here at the seminar?

— *Because of the plan of our life, fate. Why am I not at war? Because my soul, my essence does not need to experience what can be experienced there.*

— So, you are here in order to receive a certain experience. What is a personality? Personality is an experience.

— *I am certain that one chooses one's fate.*

— A human being that does not understand who he is cannot choose anything. We are now using a certain notion, a notion of the Supreme "I" that we really do not fully understand. We presume there is this Supreme "I" that sends us here to go through a certain training. This is an acceptable analogy we can work with.

— *In other words, if we did not need it, we would not be here. Is that right?*

— Yes. We need to complete a certain work here to become aware of ourselves, and we need to bring our cognitive processes to the point where we would feel what kind of work it is. I am doing this. This process is very difficult. Your thinking should become paradoxical. The conditioned mind which is one-sided and thinks in fragments is totally unaccustomed to it. I cannot pass on to you what I have to pass on using the methods that are commonly used here, because they are made for the fragmented and conditioned thinking. We, on the other hand, gathered here in order to move to a quantitatively different level of thinking and perception. This is not going to be easy.

31

— Our goal is to get to a different level. In order for us to get there, or to receive the experience, we need to pass through certain obstacles. If we don't do it now, we would not be able to move further later on, and as a result we would not achieve what our Soul requires.

Everything that can be said using words is relative

— Yes, we can say so, but only with the understanding that everything we say using words is relative. One needs to constantly remember that. If you came here with the presumption that you would hear some kind of eternal Truth with a capital "T," and hearing it from my mouth you would become the carrier of it, you are mistaken. This is not so.

This work can be done only by moving up the ladder of self-awareness step by step. I push you toward certain notions that help you in this process, but they do not represent the final, definitive Truth. The Truth is impossible to understand using the conditioned mind. **Your notion of the Truth will change in correspondence to the changes in the vibration that you would be able to accept.**

— A feeling appeared that probably contains a duality: what is right and what is wrong?

— The Truth is something that is not dual. The Truth is neither right nor wrong. We are here in quite an interesting situation and our work is quite unusual precisely because we have to deal with that illusory apparatus of notions that has been worked up by the dual conditioned mind. I have to repeat, you cannot perceive what I am discussing here using the habitual mode of perception you got so used to in schools and universities.

What is being transmitted here is energy and information. The most important topics (which appear to you that I discuss using words) in reality is being transmitted as the energy of higher vibrations. Some people have the ability to accept those vibrations while others do not.

By the way, all living creatures are tuned to a certain level of vibrations. The capacity to perceive a higher level of vibrations is a potential peculiarity of a certain category of people. I presume that this includes those people who have gathered here. I repeat, this process is not going to be easy.

Currently, we are using a certain relative model of notions about ourselves that is based on the fact that we are the Supreme "I." Your conditioned mind will tell you, "I have a Supreme "I."" Did it say so?

— *Yes.*

— It will say, "I have a car, a wife, a child, and a Supreme "I.""

— *To simplify, it will tell me that I am already a sentient being.*

— So, it is not the "i" that has the Supreme "I," but the Supreme "I" has "i" or "me."

— *I resent that. I don't like that.*

— You are the center of the Earth, and everything should belong to you. That is how you see yourself and the cosmos. People used to think that Earth stood on three elephants, and all the planets and the Sun were just rotating around it. Today, many people think that the human being is a pinnacle of nature. When nature does not give us something, we take it by force. In reality, what we call a human being is just one out of billions of forms used by the Supreme Mind to acquire experience. It is very pleasant to consider yourself to be the king of nature, but this is not so. A human being is a biological thinking machine constructed in order for different

33

civilizations, the evolutionary ways of which has not yet intersected, to connect. A human being represents a certain arena where different civilizations interact and perform their show. That is why I say that a human being does not really exist in the way we habitually perceive ourselves or other people. It is an illusion.

— *What about us sitting here, talking to and seeing each other?*

— This is an illusion perceived as reality.

— *Is it real that we sit here?*

— It is both real and not. I said it is going to be very difficult to understand, but we need to start somewhere.

— *I have my own practice of internal observation. I observe my internal question, and without blaming myself, simply tune into the situation. I feel that things are starting to move. Should I take part in the show or just observe it from the sidelines? I was always involved in this show, but it looks like I reached a peak and it is being neutralized now. I see "bad stuff" around me, but I don't blame. I perceive "good things" quietly without excitement. Sometimes I approach such emptiness, that I realize I can neither laugh nor cry. What is it?*

— I am going to return to what I discussed previously. A human being represents a certain system that has been constructed in order for certain civilizations, which otherwise would not meet, to connect. A human being is a twelve chakra system. Most people know about seven chakras. Many books are written on this topic. You can read about it. There are five more chakras that are situated outside the body. Those chakras unite us with what is outside this reality and even outside of the solar system. These higher chakras connect us to the Mind that is outside of the solar system. I am giving you a broad description of a human being make-up.

— *My mind resists. It says that this is just another concept, another religion on which I am going to build a house that will eventually collapse.*

— Exactly. I told you that everything I say is relative. I do not insist it being the Truth with a capital "T." I am telling you this to point you toward certain steps that would allow you to wake up. However, our conditioned mind does not perceive what I discuss, even in such a simplified form. It gets outraged.

Why is it outraged? Presently, I am activating a side of your personal duality of which you are not conscious. I am offering you to become aware of your opposite side, but your habitual part gets irritated. That's how the mechanism of duality is working in you.

— *What if it does not cause the irritation?*

— It means you are not yet aware of it.

— *Is it possible for there to be a total acceptance? What if there is no irritation? Does it mean something is not working?*

— We cannot talk about total acceptance because we don't know ourselves yet. It means that you cannot become aware of what was just dramatized in Andrey. You may become aware of it later. Then you will get into the state he is in right now. Every single one of us here will illustrate something to others. What happens to one here will touch everyone else. Pay attention to it. This is very important.

If you think that it is related only to Andrey, you are mistaken. This is related to everyone. This is the illustration for everyone. Using him as an example I am showing all of you how the mechanism of the dual, false personality works. He reacted to it. The fact that you did not react to it similarly does not mean you do not possess a similar mechanism. It just tells us that you are not yet aware of it.

Let me repeat. A human being is a biological, thinking, electromagnetic system created in order to interconnect different civilizations that have opposite tendencies of development. It is presumed that such a close interaction will lead to the transformation of their inherited oppositions into a new quality. In other words, out of two opposite qualities something new should arise that has a higher frequency of vibrations.

I'll give you an analogy. How do you bake a loaf of bread? You take some flour, water, eggs, yeast, and sugar. You mix them together and heat up this dough. A loaf of bread comes out of the oven consisting of all those components but has a completely different quality. What we call bread is not the flour. It is not the water or the eggs, the way those products existed previously. Combined, these ingredients assumed a totally different quality.

The spiritual development of a human being is tied to how he integrates the qualities of opposite directions that I call duality. These qualities ensure a personality of a given human being with certain essences from oppositely oriented civilizations.

— *Is the human being an antenna?*

— Yes, we can look at a human being as an antenna. I said that a human being is a twelve chakras system. Currently, a human being is not a complete human being. In the beginning, the human being was created by the form creators who were not capable of creating higher than the level of a third chakra. He was created at the level of three chakras. Notwithstanding that all the people have two hands, two legs, and one head, their chemical composition is completely different and depends on how their body was constructed.

People who have an opportunity to open the seventh or higher chakras are currently an exception. Bodies of such people are constructed by the creators of much higher levels than those who create human bodies that have only the three lowest chakras activated.

Humanity is preparing for a quantum leap, i.e. the transfer to a different state of consciousness where your perception of yourself and the surrounding life will be completely different. How does such a complicated process occur? Bodies that are capable of activating the chakras of fourth or higher levels will be able to enter the new reality.

We reviewed how the ego or false personality and the conditioned mind function. They function based on the notion of division because their perception is dual. This dual perception is a consequence of the activation of the lowest levels of the first three chakras.

What bothers people the most? It is survival. The most important thing is to survive. It can be seen easier in soldiers, because the most important thing during any war is to survive. It is the level of muladhara. It's a fight for physical survival. The second chakra is sexual war. The third chakra is fight for power. Look, those three chakras encompass practically all the scenarios we have here.

— *And what about yours?*

— It's a different scenario. In all these scenarios the ego that needs to get something for itself is present. This ego works on the level "I want it for myself." The opposite side is altruism. The appearance of the altruism by itself, i.e. doing something for someone as if for oneself, is only possible when the fourth chakra is open.

This reality acts as a sleeping gas

— The quantum leap of consciousness I discussed, or the change in the qualities of the scenarios of this reality and its transfer to a qualitatively different level of vibrations, is tied up to this process. In reality, a human being the way he is now represents an opportunity for the next quality of consciousness. However, because the activation of energy in the majority of people happens primarily on the first three chakras, we have a corresponding quality of life that is being characterized by the dual perception of the world, division, and egocentrism.

I do not say that this is bad. Our Supreme "I" sent us here to acquire life experiences precisely in these vibrations. In order for us to move to the higher levels of vibrations we need to move through the lowest levels first. No creature can increase its vibrations without going through the lowest vibrations.

Three dimensional reality is one of the lowest vibrational realities. To awaken here is a very difficult task. The number of illusions present here act as sleeping gas. It is extremely difficult to break through these illusions. One has to have very strong intent.

— *What can we compare intent to?*

— I want to emphasize that intent does not come from dual personal desires. The ego is formed in duality. It is characterized by contradictory desires. We happen to be part of the show that can be called "the illusions of dual perception." To exit this show, we have to clearly see these illusions as illusions. We have to clearly see each one of them in minute detail within ourselves. Otherwise, you are bound to remain asleep.

Simply reading different books would not get you far. It would only provide you with the illusory notion about your own awakening and make you even more aggressive toward others who are asleep. You will wage war on them. This reality is a reality of war.

A war appears as a result of a man being in a divided state: one of his parts is at war with another, but because one side is not aware of the other, shadow part in oneself, one projects it onto somebody else and gets into a war with him or her—in reality with oneself.

There are only wars here. Regardless of whether you have a gun in your hand or not, regardless of whether you are in the war zone or not, these wars are everywhere: at home, at work, on a bus, etc. The war with oneself is the essence of our experiencing the state of division. One can only exit this war by becoming fully aware of oneself. That is precisely what I am offering to you.

But do you have this intent? I repeat that the intent is coming from the part of you that is not dual, i.e. from your Supreme "I." But the illusion of division here is perceived as the only reality.

Let's talk about the notion of a human being. I said upfront that a human being, the way he sees himself now and the way others see him, is just a fruit of a dual perception. His main task is the accumulation of the experiences of living through the opposite sides of personal qualities.

Everything that can be attributed to the physical plane: body, name, and different roles (man—woman, mother—father, daughter—son) are simply certain methods of acquiring experience. Therefore, the main question is what kind of experience you came to Earth to acquire.

— *Who are "you"? Is it a human being that is comprised of multiple personalities or the Supreme "I"? Who wants to receive this experience?*

— We were talking about the presence of Supreme "I." But one can only start feeling oneself as Supreme "I" after exiting those notions about oneself as a personality. It is one thing to hear from someone about the Supreme "I," and another thing to learn that you were sent here by your Supreme "I." It is a totally different thing to feel yourself as the Supreme "I." But you will only feel yourself as the Supreme "I" if and when the energies of the Supreme "I" and the lower "i" synchronize.

How do you understand what the Supreme "I" is? For example, your "i" in the fourth chakra is higher than compared to your "i" in the third chakra. A human being is a twelve chakras system. So what is your Supreme "I"? And where should one look for God?

— *Inside oneself.*

— Inside oneself. Then the "i" on the level of the eighth chakra is god in relationship to me on the level of the fifth chakra. But it is all me. How can my consciousness enter the chakras of the higher levels? It can only be done by increasing the level of vibration of my consciousness. Otherwise "i" would not be able to synchronize with the vibrational level of these higher chakras. While "i" can have ideas of "How to become the Supreme "I,"" "i" cannot realize them unless "i" increases the quality of its consciousness. At any given moment, "i" can only correspond to the level of vibrations of consciousness at which "i" happens to be.

How was a human being created? In particular, how did the liver, the kidney, the arms, the legs, and everything else appear? What do you think? How did all of this appear and who created this?

— *We created it all.*

— Did we create it ourselves? In a way this is so, but do you understand who those "We" are?

— *The essence.*

— What kind of essence?

— *The essence that is smarter than us.*

— We are talking about the "Supreme Mind" of a human being, but is there the "Supreme Mind" of the Earth? Is there a "Supreme Mind" of the Sun? Is there a "Supreme Mind" of the Galaxy? Is there a "Supreme Mind" of the Universe?

— *If we consider ourselves to be the microcosm, we were probably created by those who are in the macrocosm.*

— And what is "We"? What do we mean when we say, "We were created"? Who created our body, or our spacesuit?

— *A human being created a space suite. It looks like a human being has created his own body.*

— No, not a human being. Aside from a human being, there are billions of other creatures that possess completely different types of consciousness and group together into Group Minds. We were saying that a cell is a microcosm, while a Solar system is a macrocosm, but the principals of their organization are the same. So, who created those cells that united in certain organs, which then united into a certain body that we call a human body? These cells were created by different civilizations whose representatives receive their own experience through what they have created. A physical body of a human being represents a certain playground created by certain civilizations in order to receive certain experiences.

— *Do they cooperate?*

— I would call it the fight and the unity of opposites. It is a dynamic system that is based on multiple contradictions. These contradictions, interacting with each other, should transform into a new quality, into the mind of a higher quality. A human being was created in order to solve this particular task.

— *I thought there was only one Creator, and inside every human being there was a Supreme "I," a part of this Creator.*

— Every one of us has certain notions about ourselves that most frequently are illusory. You can have a notion of God and Evil, but most important for you is why you did not get a promotion this year or why your boyfriend is not proposing to you.

Occasionally, I meet with people who read my books. I ask them, "Why did you come?" They say, "I have read your books." "And?" – I ask. The reply is, "I am interested in getting acquainted with you. What other interesting ideas do you have? What kind of cigarettes do you smoke? How strong are your glasses?" I answer them and they go home satisfied.

— *They might not be satisfied.*

— They cannot get satisfied. When one lives in a state of separation, one cannot experience any satisfaction except the one that leads to dissatisfaction.

As you can see, I am holding the line of our conversation not on what interests your personality. I am transferring the conversation to a sphere that is higher than the personality. I understand that your conditioned mind wants to send me and what I say to hell, because I am not using the cognitive patterns accepted here. What I discuss irritates your conditioned mind. Moreover, I talk about things that do not enter the narrow borders of notions your conditioned mind has pertaining to God, other people, civilization, etc. You are

42

getting uncomfortable. You cannot be comfortable. I am talking about your conditioned mind. Your conditioned mind is getting uncomfortable.

I understand what kind of difficulties you are going through. Look, half of this group consists of new people and another half has been here for a while. One may think that I should start from the beginning, but I don't do that. It is impossible to start from the beginning here, in our process, as we move with a constant acceleration. The next group will be ready for a stronger push. I see those who came as those who can move at a high speed. I am not a school teacher who comes to the first grade class repeating the same lesson over and over again.

Every one of you here assumes himself to be the center of the Earth. Your personalities have those assumptions. I destroy those assumptions. I say things to you that cannot get incorporated into the narrow limits of the notions commonly accepted here. Moreover, things I say contradict those notions. This leads to the appearance of very difficult states in you. On a personal level, you will experience aggression, irritation, and rejection. However, the parts of you that are of higher vibrations know and understand what, in reality, happens here. They will be in a completely different state. So, what parts of you are you going to orient yourself toward? I am producing a roller-coaster for you in order to create an opportunity for you to become aware of yourself as *something* outside of your personality. That *something* in you understands what is going on here very well, but you are not aware of it. I keep telling you that a human being, the way he imagines himself to be, is an illusion. I question every single notion you have about yourself. I question the notions you consider to be self-evident.

The main question is what you consider to be real. It is not simply an intellectual knowledge and not a question of believing me. You may believe me now, but you will not believe me tomorrow. What I discuss should be thoroughly lived through by you. You should get to the level of vibrations this information is coming from. Only then will you say: "Yes, this is so."

— *Duality. Again I am choosing between the high and the low vibrations. It's a contradiction.*

— Correct. We are going to go through a very difficult step on our pathway to ourselves, which happens to be dual. You will experience serious fluctuations in your states, from condemning me to blaming yourselves. You will condemn me for what I say and for what you do not understand. You will scream that I talk nonsense. Then you will feel guilty because you don't understand me. One state will lead to and change to another, but in reality, you feel both of them simultaneously. However, the conditioned mind does not allow you to process and understand it. The main task of our process at the present time is to start to think paradoxically. **Paradoxical thinking is thinking that comes from the simultaneous vision of dualities of which your personality consists. This is what self-investigation is. You need to start to investigate yourself in the paradox of duality.** I am setting certain signposts that are necessary for this self-investigation. Otherwise, you will remain within the illusions, perceiving them as reality. This is neither good nor bad. This is simply the indicator of the level of vibration of your consciousness. **Perhaps you still need to continue to accumulate the experience of war in the dual perception of the world. However, if you are ready to exit this dual perception, you will need to become fully aware of your survival**

44

experience and leave it with gratitude. This will lead to changes in the notions you have about yourself. The notions you have right now are one-sided and lead you to experience this war inside of you. Again, I am not saying that this is bad. This is experience. Without going through and experiencing these lower vibrations you cannot move forward. You can only move forward when you fully integrate this experience, feel it, and become aware of it. We will work and become aware of all those experiences. It will change not only our mental, but also our emotional notions of ourselves.

Talk and be aware of what you are saying

— We did an experiment during which I asked you to discuss what statements pertaining to you irritate you. Those are the notions about yourself that you will need to see and to accept in yourself. You will need to clearly see all your virtues and, corresponding to them, shortcomings as something that you are made of. To see yourself as a whole means to understand and to accept the dualities, i.e. the contradictions of your personality. If you consider yourself to be kind and insist on it, I will show you your mean side. Unless you see and accept this opposite side of your kindness, you will not be able to move to the next level of quality of vibrations of consciousness, because the next level of consciousness appears as a result of the synthesis and integration of the oppositions in yourself, i.e. in your personality. When the quality that you are conscious of in yourself and the quality that you perceive as opposite and project onto others are suddenly seen by you as a whole, as two sides of one coin, you will experience enlightenment.

That is very important for practical work on yourself. I just gave you a broader picture for seeing yourself, because that is what is necessary for practical work. I only give here what is necessary for practical work. If I discuss something that appears to be theoretical to you, it is necessary for practical work.

You cannot perform the work on awareness and integration of opposite sides of yourself without understanding, or at least getting in touch with new notions of yourself. The majority of you would take what I have just said as just another intellectual idea, just another point of view. Perhaps those ideas oppose your picture of yourself and of the creation completely. But what I say dramatizes your current notions by pushing you to see something else. That is the major point of my work.

I would ask you to bring forward what you feel. By discussing what you feel, you start to see your personality from another side. Otherwise, you are not aware of it. Talk about what you feel. Don't be afraid to insult me. It is impossible and laughable. Don't be afraid to insult yourself, as it is equally laughable.

— *I feel tension and relaxation at the same time.*

— Where? The more you talk about your personality, the faster your transformation will occur. You can be silent. I am not going to force anyone, but then the effect will be significantly slower.

— *I feel my chest expanding and some tension in the heart chakra. I feel I am ready to fly.*

— *I simultaneously feel emptiness and direction inside.*

— *I have a dragging sensation. When I look at you, certain images appear; sometimes I see an older man and sometimes I see a scientist. Suddenly, everything becomes fluid. Reality shifts. Vibration is felt all*

46

over the body. When thoughts are present, those sensations disappear. When thoughts disappear, sensations appear again. Right before I decided to speak up about it, I developed palpitations. I decided not to talk and to allow other people to say something first. My heart started to palpitate even harder. But now, when I expressed myself, it is slowing down.

— I want to add something. I am new here. I too saw images. I thought I saw them because of the tension of my gaze. I think I saw what I was not supposed to see.

— I had similar thoughts.

— When you look at me, you see yourself. You need to understand that this division—I am separate and he is separate—is the major attribute of duality. You can only see in me what you can see in yourself.

I said that a human being is a certain biological thinking machine constructed for the evolution of consciousness. The essences that occupy the lowest overtones of chakras and realize themselves in such way do not want to lose this opportunity. Let me use an analogy here. Imagine you are living in a house, and suddenly someone comes and announces that some other people, people of higher vibrations will live here from now on. You start to fight for your house. This will happen to you, because the entrance of new vibrations is accompanied by a strong resistance from the old habits, habits that were worked up by these essences. If you identify with such habitual feelings as jealousy, guilt, fear, condemnation, you will not be able to move to where we are moving.

You are satisfied with the show you play. Actually, it is not you who are satisfied, but those essences that use your body to play that show. When you are totally identified with them, you can't do anything. Only by crossing the level of the third chakra to the fourth chakra, you will start to see what

47

happened and what happens in your life from the side. Then you will become capable of conducting self-investigation, the essence of which is observation. It's the observation of those scripts that are being acted out by you. Are they acted out by you? This is a big question that will lead you to better understand who, in reality, you are.

— *I want to add something. During the last couple of years, I occasionally see some creatures. I thought it was an illusion, an image, a smell or a sound. I don't even know if it was a dream or not. Now, after I heard what you have just said, I have started to become aware of things that are real.*

— When I say that a body is a product of the creativity of certain civilizations that would simply decompose after your death, you identify yourself with your body.

— *After the death of my body?*

— Yes, after the death of your physical body. In reality, there is no such thing as death. Death does not exist.

— *Is death just a transfer?*

— Yes. If I consider myself to be the physical body, then I am afraid of losing it—in exactly the same way I am afraid to lose my personality. But I will show you that you are not your personality either. So, who are you?

— *I did not hear anything new during today's meeting. In the information you presented, I saw many mental constructs, but there was also something else—I experienced something new. I listened, and at one point I became aware that if I listen and get surprised, then...*

— *Maybe it has already been experienced?*

— I doubt it.

— *Perhaps this is an illusion on my part, but what you were saying about chakras, I think I had certain sensations pertaining to them. But many things are still seen just as conceptions in my mind. You see, I am looking at you, and at certain moments I see a light shadow behind you. I*

48

see a whole human being that moves. I never experienced spiritual visions, but something inside me tells me that this is quite real. These episodes did not cause any resistance.

— Please, express the most important part of what you want to say.

— *I want to say that this picture is not true in certain basic premises; it is not true in a certain perception of it that I have.*

— The most important thing that can happen to you now can be expressed as a transfer from "I don't know that I don't know" to "I know that I don't know." Having an enormous number of different presumptions born out of multiple illusions, you cannot understand something that is not illusory. This is what Jesus expressed when he said, "Do not pour new wine into the old wineskins." With the help of awareness, one can clean up one's mind from many illusory notions that one considers real and are based on how one acts. This is a very important but also a very difficult process. In order to do that, one has to catch, feel thoroughly, and start to understand the basic idea of self-investigation. I have touched upon it briefly here.

We are going to work with it. This is the first meeting of our group, which consists of both old and new members. The most important moment for new people is to admit that what they understand about themselves and about the world is **relative**. Your notions may change if you have the intention of acquiring a new experience. If you continue to identify with your personality, the process of transformation will not be possible; you will continue to pacify yourself with the habitual for your personality illusions. If you like it, you can continue to do so, but you will not be able to remain here, because this process presupposes an undoing of what you considered to be yourself, i.e. the exit out of the old notions of what you

49

considered to be yourself. Everyone has these notions, but at the moment, no one can describe them. My question "Who are you?" was not answered.

The way we perceive ourselves and others is an illusion. Our body is not ours. It consists of billions of cells collected in organs, created by different civilizations to experience in this body what they need to experience. What we consider to be our personality is also not ours. It represents a number of certain creatures that use our body in order to experience what they need to experience. The experiences they get on the level of first three chakras are survival, sexuality, and power. All types of this experience are dual and lead to suffering, because they do not allow us to see things as they are in reality.

Living through this experience occurs in a state of total identification. Transfer to the fourth chakra will allow you to take the first step toward an opportunity to investigate reality as it is. This is a step you need to take, but it is connected to the beginning of seeing the illusory nature of what you used to consider to be the only reality. We are going to work with many illusions. Our work is to see illusions as illusions, and the way these illusions operate. Personality, which creates its own life, happens to be one of these illusions.

— *I am experiencing a very unusual sensation for me. I have chronic pain in my groin, which fluctuates in intensity. I have an interesting relationship with it. I always wanted to get rid of this pain. I used different methods before, but now I just sit here observing it without any desire to stop it. I am also experiencing a certain perturbation mixed with excitement. I am not sure how to express it. It is very unusual.*

— **Transfer from war to observation is the major outcome of spiritual development. The war is provided, occurs, continues, and supported by the internal**

50

separation of the conditioned mind and personality. It is precisely this internal separation of the personality that gives birth to every day drama. This reality is a huge drama theater. Drama is a collision of opposites, and the more dramatic your personal show, the better actor you are. That explains the continuous suffering of people; drama actors should suffer. That is the part of one's show. Suffering is necessary for an actor of any drama. What kind of a drama actor could we have without suffering? What kind of a drama could we have without suffering?

Our main goal is to exit the drama of suffering. The war we observe in our external life is a reflection of our internal state of separation, when one part of us is fighting another, opposite part of us. But because we do not accept the part we fight with as ours, we project that part onto other people and start to fight them. We condemn them. However, in condemning them, we also feel guilty for this condemnation. In order not to feel this guilt, we condemn others even more. The mechanism of a dramatic show is built on condemnation and guilt. How and what do you condemn?

— *Are you saying that every time I condemn someone, I really condemn myself, but in a different face, in a different human being?*

— Correct. You condemn yourself, but for what reason do you condemn yourself? The reason can be extrapolated and seen through the external people you condemn.

— *Due to the fact that many new people showed up today, the seminar did not go the way I expected it to go.*

— Not the way you are used to.

— *Perhaps, not the way I am used to, it is irrelevant.*

— No, it is quite relevant.

— Well, not the way ... because this irritation was building up. My mind understands that everything is right, but my emotions are not willing to obey. My logic does not work. My emotions build up. My neighbor reinforced this irritation, and I spilled everything I was building up on him.

— You did it so sincerely that at a certain point you became ashamed.

— It seems funny now, but you are right.

— Funny, but very sad. And that will continue until you start to sort out the dualities that create these situations. One part of you condemns another part of you, which you project onto me. I ask every one of you to express why he or she condemns me. You condemned me today, and you did it quite a few times. Let me put it differently: for what reasons do you condemn me? It is easier to sort out one's own condemnation through the external screen. Looking inside, you cannot say much about yourself, at least for now. This reality is created in such a way that our internal world is projected outside. Now, as I have talked more than anybody else today, and some of you may have disagreed with certain things, I would ask you to express your condemnations.

A dialogue with a teacher

— I was probably the source of that irritation that later on was transmitted to the group, and everything went askew.

— You came, and you brought the whole group to the state of vibrations in which you happened to be.

— I am not the center of the Universe. I don't consider myself to be.

— You are lying. You just declared precisely that. You are saying that it was you who brought irritation to the group.

— *You know, one can interpret another's words differently, saying that this is relative and that is relative, that one is relative and one's words are relative.*

— You are condemning me right now, right? I was asking for a specific condemnation.

— *I am going to get specific now.*

— I think you have already said everything.

— *Did I?*

— You made a prelude. Now you are making a prelude to a prelude. What do you feel toward me right now?

— *I feel that you do not correspond to my image of a teacher. I came and I saw it. I was brought here by a chain of events.*

— I asked you to specifically state what you condemn me for. You have said it, but you do not comprehend that.

— *You constantly interrupt.*

— Yes, and that is just a miniscule portion of what I am going to do. That is simply a gentle stroking. What irritates you about me? You are so nice. You cannot say, cannot confess that something irritates you about me. Is that so?

— You are an asshole.

— Okay. I need specifics. Why?

— *Something happened to me. I was in a good mood…and you, you asshole, you won't let me talk.*

— What are you condemning me for? I asked you a specific question.

— *In order to answer specifically, one has to backtrack a bit.*

— You are backtracking from a backtrack that leads to backtracking from a previous backtrack. I asked you to say specifically what irritates you about me.

— *The image of a teacher of the light that sits here cursing people, and nobody dares to reply.*

53

— Excellent. You could have said, "Don't mess with my loving you, with such an image of you that I want to see." This is an excellent illustration of the main drama of which the lives of many people consists.

— *I found your book. I saw the situation that happened to me through your book.*

— You love my books, but you do not love the author. You thought I was different. You discovered me the way I am, and you don't like me.

— *You don't even want to know what people think of you.*

— In the same way, you do not want to know what you think of yourself.

— *Why do you ask if you do not care?*

— It does not matter to me, but it matters to you. We gathered here in order to investigate ourselves. We did not gather here to elevate or downgrade my image. The more you are going to elevate me, the more you are going to hate me. That is what Jesus showed. To call me a teacher of the light or a teacher of darkness is the same, as both are one. You can't get to the light unless you know what darkness is. Light and darkness are just two sides of one coin.

Darkness is what you do not know about yourself. That is why I am a teacher of darkness as I sort out what you do not know about yourself. That's paradoxical thinking. How does your brain react to it? Light can only be brought to darkness. If you shine a flashlight during a bright daylight, it would not change much. But if you start using it in the dark, you would see what you could not see without it.

— *I found the answers to all my questions in your book. I used to say, "God, thank you for that man. Thank you for what he wrote." It's all written there, everything that happened to me. I recall my whole life, all the situations that happened to me. I found the answers to the questions I could not even get close to.*

— The author of this book sits here, and we would condemn him right now.

— *I am surprised. Why did I come here?*

— After a strong enchantment, a similarly strong disenchantment appears. It is precisely in this disenchantment that you are currently sitting. You passed the stage of getting uphill. Now, you are going to go downhill.

— *I do not understand why I sense those sensations inside.*

— It happens because every personality is dual. Behind love stands hate, and the stronger the love, the stronger the hate will be. Until you are ready to observe both love and hate without emotions, you will not understand who you really are. You received a portion of pleasure, but now I will give you a portion of displeasure in order for you to see in displeasure pleasure, and in pleasure displeasure. This is the essence of our process. That is why I repeat that my books are just business cards. I use them the same way fisherman uses fishhooks. I use them for fishing. But when the fish is caught and brought up to the shore, it experiences a completely different state.

— *Something happens to me and I find the answers in the books later on, or I read something in the books and the answer comes next.*

— Okay. You have read the books and found some answers to your questions. When you came to the author of the books, he brought up more difficult questions. Now you are irritated because you do not have the answers to those new, more difficult questions. You can only get the answers by becoming aware of yourself. You cannot get them by reading books. It's easy with a book. You read a book, enjoy it, put it under a pillow, and fall asleep. You can pray to a book. A book cannot upset you. It lays there and if you get bored by it, you can throw it out. It is easy with a book. It is challenging with the author.

— *You wrote about it in your books.*

— Exactly. And you said you understood that. Did you?

— *It appears that to understand and to become aware of something are two different things. Everyone has a certain understanding.*

— Understanding is a result of awareness. Awareness is an opportunity to see love and hate as two sides of one coin. Attraction and repulsion are also two sides of one coin. There are many other dualities. The voltage between the opposite sides of these dualities creates a structure of your life script. You need to start working with it. You need to become aware of these dualities and to investigate them in your personality.

Thank you for your dislike of me

— Thank you for telling me how distasteful I am to you. Previously, you were going through a state of an enchantment, and now you are going through the opposite state—irritation, dislike. We live in a world of dual illusions. Usually what happens here is not what you have expected. Expectations are born from the assumptions of one of the two directors of your personality. The other, opposite director, acts subconsciously. If one of them loves, another hates. Two of them represent two sides of one's personality. Neither one of them is bad. Both of them are necessary. So, if you were to tell me that I am good, I would say, "No, I am bad, and I am going to be bad in what you consider me to be good. That is why you are not going to tell me anything new about yourself. However, you can say a lot about yourself to yourself, and that is what I am pushing you to do.

This reality is activated by the notions of the conditional, dual mind and I practically bring them to one point. When you start to do it, no one will be able to offend or insult you, you will move to a completely different qualitative state of consciousness. It is impossible to explain this quality of consciousness by using words. There are no words for it, and to talk about what has not been lived through is senseless. We can only talk about the experiences that have been lived through. In order to approach the state of integration of the opposites, one has to complete the work of self-investigation. That's what we are doing, even though it is not simple.

— *When we discussed today what irritates whom, I saw myself being irritated by my own stupidity. I was constantly told as a kid that I was stupid. It used to always cause a state of depression in me. Suddenly, I understood that I experience great pleasure precisely because I get a confirmation from the part which considers itself stupid.*

— Exactly. But in order to feel stupid, you need somebody smart. Pint, for example. You can position me to be very smart, and then with smart Pint on a background, you would be stupid. That's precisely what you need, as in such a case you would live through the whole gamma of feelings connected to your stupidity.

— *One can get so much kaif* out of it.*

— Well, everyone is in it. Everyone would try to drag me and everyone else into their own dramatic scripts and shows. You, for example, would create situations leading to you feeling stupid.

— *In order to receive two states, pleasure and displeasure, simultaneously.*

— Yes. As personalities, we are used to playing the shows of a dramatic character. Becoming aware of our personality allows us to move toward a show of a completely different quality. However, you can only approach that other show by becoming aware of the ways you create your current dramas.

Now, I will ask you to express your attitude to what you have just observed.

— *Complete mess in my head.*

— *I like what happens here.*

— *Unusual.*

— *A completely different internal sensation. I can perceive and live differently.*

— *Excitement. I have a feeling that something burst. Something heavy and constricting has burst.*

— *I did not have any expectations of what would happen, only internal attention.*

— *For a long time, I did not experience a sensation of a strong heartbeat as a result of what happened in the group. Usually, there is an excitement before the seminar, when one knows new people are going to appear. Today there was a sensation that when one enters one's head, it starts to hurt, and when one looks at people seeing the light that comes from each and every one, there is such a sensation that the heart is working on a completely different level. There is a sensation of warmth coming from everyone. I feel that every heart was open irrespective of how the mind worked.*

— In the world of illusions everything is dual. Find an opposition in yourself to what you have just said and confirm it. Your conditioned mind may say that I enforce the division. That's right, and I will continue to enforce it in order for you to see it. **To divide in order to see and to see in order to connect is the main rule of our process.** In the dark room, all the cats appear grey and you cannot say what color they are in reality. That is how the human being perceives his internal world. Everything is grey.

58

Certain situations will be created here which will strongly separate one part of you from another, the opposite part of you, creating an opportunity to see the dualities of your personality. When you see them, you will connect them and move to another quality of consciousness. This will happen, not thanks to the conditioned mind, but in spite of it.

* Kaif or Kif – from Arabic *kayf* pleasure.
Any drug or agent that when smoked is capable of producing a euphoric condition.
The euphoric condition produced by smoking marijuana.

CHAPTER 2
THE RESTAURANT OF FEAR. OUR PERSONALITY IS DUAL.

◆•◆•◆•◆•◆•◆•◆•◆•◆•◆•◆•◆•◆•◆•◆•◆•

— I hate myself for searching for a system of coordinates of notions and beliefs where I would be comfortable. I would find them and fall asleep there again. I would put awareness under my pillow, cover myself with dualities, and get very comfortable in this system of coordinates. Prior to that, something was bothering me. I was not comfortable. Yesterday I noticed what a lover of life I am. Many of us died here yesterday, but today they are sitting here prettier than ever.

— One should die every moment.

— I long for life. In reality, I am not willing to die. I am a walking dead, but I can only be reborn if I die. Everyone died yesterday, and everyone is different today.

— We will have to die again today.

— We were talking about us getting born and dying. Suddenly, a thought appeared that we give birth here. We give birth in pain and suffering. In order for us to learn to give birth in happiness and pain-free, we need to learn to give birth in pain.

— Excellent. It has started. Here is my resonance to what you just said. Let me tell you about myself. I am a mirror. You

61

have probably noticed that I behave quite differently. I behave differently with different people and with the same person depending on which side he or she shows. **What can this give you? This allows you to see yourself. A new woman that left yesterday was not satisfied. She was condemning me, but she did not see this condemnation. I confronted her with her constant apologizing. Why was she apologizing? She was blocking her aggression. Officially, she is expressing apologies, but factually she is condemning. Later on she started to show condemnation. We offered her an opportunity to become aware of this condemnation, but she was not ready for it.**

The basic thing that happens here is awareness. Everyone is involved with his or her tendencies and roles. When one is completely identified with them, one simply projects them onto others. I emphasize again, **my function is to reflect what you express in order for you to see it.** That is very important for everyone to understand.

I said that you will both hate and love me. You will experience completely opposite feelings toward me, because I constantly stimulate you to express your feelings. **Understanding occurs not as a result of receiving certain information or by your conditioned mind memorizing it, but by living through your experiences while maintaining a state of awareness. Understanding appears as the result of you living through a new experience and its juxtaposition onto the old one. In order to receive a new experience, new knowledge is needed, and this new knowledge needs to be lived through.**

You received your old knowledge of life during your upbringing. Those are old parental programs that are fixed in you emotionally. Therefore, everyone carries his

own painful moments that maintain these programs. You are just working these programs up. You cannot change them unless you become fully aware of them in yourself.

Our task is to become aware of these programs and to exit them. One can only exit them by **becoming fully aware** of them, not by simply acquiring some information. You can receive information about things such as UFOs, extraterrestrials, the Supreme "I," and many other things offered by esoteric literature, but that would not change the structure of your fate in any way, i.e. the structure of your personality.

Here we have a practical task to transform ourselves. This transformation involves changing the notions we have about ourselves. It is only possible to do so by becoming fully aware of who we are now. If you don't do it, nothing new will happen to you. You cannot receive new information without reviewing and revising the old one. To put it simply, you receive something new only to the degree of changes in the old.

The process of transformation of the old is the process of the synthesis of dualities. This reality is built on the principle of duality. Opposite qualities or opposite civilizations interact here. But I don't want to look at it now from the point of view of different civilizations, as your mind will hallucinate on those abstract notions. I will only concentrate on the point of view of personality changes. In order for you to see what I discuss in a broader, cosmic context, you need to learn your personality very well. That work consists of step-by-step awareness of your old programs.

Any given personality is built on duality. For example, strength and weakness are two opposite sides of one duality. In order to appraise one side, you need to lean on its opposite side. Can you remove your weakness? Can you remove one side of the coin and keep the coin itself? It is impossible. **How do you know that you are strong? You know it based on the fact that someone is weaker than you. You can only be strong in relation to somebody who is weaker. But you will be weaker in relation to someone who is stronger. He, in turn, will be weaker in relation to someone who is even stronger.**

In reality, you will never become the strongest man, as there will always be someone stronger than you. You will never become the richest man, as there will always be someone richer than you. You can't become anyone your personality wants you to become as there will always be someone that will top you. This, by the way, is limitless on both the positive and negative sides. This is how every personality is built.

Whatever your personality lusts for and invests your energy to achieve, always has the opposite side. Do you agree?

— *Yes.*

— You should always compare everything I say with your own experience. I am not discussing abstract things here. This is practical work. When you compare what we discuss here with your personal experience, you will see that power and weakness are qualities of one scale. You will understand that while being strong, you are simultaneously equally weak. Weakness is not something negative. Strength is not something positive. Positive and negative are just technical terms analogous to plus and minus in a battery.

Being handsome, you are equally ugly. Being smart, you are equally stupid. However, the conditioned mind cannot see two sides of duality simultaneously. It wants to see only the positive side of it. For bad boys and girls it is the negative side, and they are fixated on it, just as good boys and girls are fixated on the positive side. Try to say to a bad boy that he is good. He would have an explosion similar to the explosion of a good boy if you were to tell him he is bad. These are two different directions, but the mechanism is the same.

Paradoxical thinking appears as a result of simultaneously seeing the opposites as being just two parts of one scale. I am teaching you paradoxical thinking now. This knowledge should be lived through by you; it should become yours experientially. By simply listening to it, you will not get it. You need to live through it. You need to experience yourself as both weak and strong, accepting both sides of one coin. You need to experience yourself as handsome and ugly, smart and stupid, spiritual and material, highest and lowest. You need to experience everything yourself and to accept it.

We see that certain dualities are common for everyone. Take, for example, the duality spiritual—material. This duality concerns all of us gathered here. By starting to live through dualities and starting to connect them, you receive a quality of mindfulness that will allow you to understand what I discuss. Then it will not be something abstract for you. It will be something you will feel and experience.

The essence of our process is to connect the mind and the heart, and to experience it. Knowledge that has been lived through turns into understanding. **In my terminology, understanding is a synthesis of new knowledge and new experience.** This is going to be a new understanding in relationship to the old understanding. If you are not aware of the state you are currently in, you do not have a starting point from which to transfer to another state. In this case, your notions of "old" and "new" would both be illusory.

To transfer to another quality of yourself is to transfer to another quality of thinking and experiencing. A new quality of perceiving yourself appears as a result of internal transmutation of opposite sides of dual qualities. In this reality, the understanding of two Godly qualities occurs as a result of passing through different levels of their development. The first quality is Godly Love-Wisdom, and the second quality is Godly Will of the Mind. One quality is a ray moving up, another—a ray moving down. Will of the Mind is an ascending ray. Love-Wisdom is a descending ray.

The system of chakras presents those qualities: first, muladhara—the will of the mind; second, svadhistana—love-wisdom; third is will of the mind again; fourth—love-wisdom; fifth—will of the mind; sixth—love-wisdom. The seventh chakra—sahasrara—connects the qualities that have been worked up during the synthesis of those two main qualities on different levels of preceding chakras; it provides an opportunity of exiting the limits of earthly experience. Further up lays the exit to the galactic level. It is pointless to discuss it now, but this is a general scheme of things.

The development of these two opposite qualities occurs as a result of the interaction of two opposite civilizations. We can call them civilizations of the Dark Ring and civilizations of the Light Ring. Your understanding of this information will occur as a result of your working through many opposite sides of yourself. In particular, your understanding of a human being as a bio-thinking machine that was created by the creators of Dark and Light Rings will happen only as a result of your work of uniting dualities inside yourself.

That is why the major accent is made on the work with dualities. Doing this work you start to increase the qualities of the functioning of your chakras. That leads you to develop a stronger interest in this information, which will become not abstract, but working information for you.

— *Can I say something, or should I be silent?*

— Do you talk only in order not to be silent? If you want to be silent, be silent. If you have something to say, say it.

— *Today I figured out that you stimulate us to break out of our beliefs. I felt it very strongly during the first day of the seminar when you inviteed us to hit someone on the face while simultaneously trying to feel what he or she was feeling in the process. I found a man and started to look at him. I experienced complete confusion. I did not know what to do. I was blown away. Suddenly, a decision jumped out of nowhere. The way I understand it now, you need to kick one's props—those convictions upon which one stands—from under him. A decision was made, but I was not sure in myself. The process was going on, emotions were building up, and suddenly I just dropped this person to the floor. I was sitting there thinking about why I did what I did. It would be so much simpler just to hit him as it usually happens in life—who will hit whom first. It was an optimal solution at the time.*

To hit, in order to revive

— The optimal solution for what? What did you want to do to your partner?

— *I understood, I needed to hit her hard.*

— Maybe you understood that you have to kill her? Then, the optimal solution is to hit her as hard as possible.

— *We can say so.*

— So, simply to kill her?

— *Well, not to kill, but …*

— But to injure.

— *That was an assignment. That is how I perceived it.*

67

— If I were to distribute knives here and tell you to cut each other up, would you do it?

— *I don't know. I am in some kind of a blur.*

— And who knows? This is the way wars get started. Someone says, "Enemies are over there. Grab your weapons. Get up. Go and kill them. This is a holy war."

— *That is precisely how I perceived the situation.*

— Exactly. You perceived it in accordance with your level of consciousness. At this level, one needs to destroy others to survive. Correct?

— *Yes.*

— And you are waiting for the order to destroy. The order is given, and destruction of the enemy starts. When I invite you to hit each other on the face, externally it appears as a fight without rules. I use this method, but the meaning I put on it is totally different from yours. I use this method because in the emotionally dead states that occur as a result of previously received painful experiences, the only method to break through the emotional defenses is to create a strong shock.

To hit another human being on the face, feeling at the same time what he feels, produces exactly that kind of a shock. I offer this in the situations when the armors of your emotional defenses are very strong. That is the case now. Someone needs to be gently stroked, another needs to be hit. He does not perceive stroking. He needs a hit of such a strength that he would feel. If he is dead, he would not even notice a gentle stroke. Imagine that your whole body lost its sensitivity. If I were to touch you, you would not even feel it. But hit with a hammer, perhaps you would feel something. It means that the threshold of your sensitivity is so high that you need to be hurt in order to feel.

For example, people say they love each other. They get married, and then they start to kick and hurt each other. This is their way of loving. It is a lower level of consciousness that factually destroys what it loves, i.e. strong destructive forces operate there. In this case, so called love is destruction. Many people live like this. With the increase in the frequency of vibrations of your consciousness you will not be able to even imagine hitting or killing someone. But for certain levels of consciousness, fighting is what one needs to occupy oneself with if one, so called, loves another human being.

— *Can I say something now? Our topic is "Love—Hate." We are saying that another human being's attitude toward us reflects our own attitude about ourselves, and one sort of agrees with the fact that this is me but does not feel it. Yesterday's episode represents a good example of what I do. I saw the pain and suffering to which we give birth when we hate or physically hurt others. I consider yesterday's episode to be a good lesson. I felt it. I was not hurting yesterday, but now I am hurting. Yesterday after the seminar, I thought about my hatred toward my partner. I was trying to figure it out, and I realized I loved him. But what was irritating me? Why did I hate him? I started to count his qualities. Then I said, "But this is me," and I started to look for these qualities in myself. And a strange picture appeared. It seems that the same qualities I hate him for, I praise in myself, considering them to be my virtues. That is how I understand duality.*

— Our virtues are continuations of our deficiencies. Like hot water and cold water, they represent one scale. Cold water is not inferior to hot water: both are necessary. But what does one do internally? One separates them, saying one is bad and he hates it, and another is good—he loves it.

— *"Love—Hate" came out of the duality "Good—Bad."*

— The duality "Love—Hate" is how One Unconditional Love manifests itself in the reality of low vibrations.

69

Everything here is created by division, i.e. by the distortion of the ray of Unconditional Love. Unconditional Love is expressed here in duality "Love—Hate." Try cutting river in two. It is impossible. But human beings do precisely that, insisting on one thing being good, and another bad. The bad thing we condemn, and feel righteous. This is a consequence of divided perception.

So, a human being fights himself, not understanding it. Then it returns back to him, but he does not see that he himself is a source of this consequence. This is extremely important to see. What I do to another is what I do to myself, but in order to see it, you need to feel. You need to feel what another human being is feeling when you hit him. That's the way to combine two sides of the duality "Love—Hate" in yourself.

— Yesterday a situation played out when two people were standing and one was saying to another, "Hit me! Hit me!" The opponent was saying, "No, I will not hit you." The first one was getting crazy. "Hit me, hit me!" And the answer was again, "No, I will not hit you." Does it mean that the equal insult and resentment are created by inactivity?

— The victim is screaming, "Hurt me! Be an oppressor! Harass me!" And the best way of doing it is in not doing it. This is what being practiced in sado-masochistic relationships. From the holistic level - both the sadist and the masochist are the same, both receive what they want. A victim happens to be an equal oppressor, and an oppressor an equal victim.

— Yesterday when I was slapped on the face, I experienced shock, and then some garbage started to come out. Today after lunch I started to laugh. I saw my lifeless body that is hidden in the hole. It is being pulled by the tail, but it does not want to come out. The state when I was slapped up a bit and brought to my senses was a great state. At a certain

70

moment, I started to laugh at myself, understanding what kind of comedy or tragedy I was playing. In reality, it is both funny and disgusting at the same time. And a question appeared. I have experienced difficult states that shook me up quite a bit, but then time passed and I entered a habitual society of people—the usual, the gray. The same dream slowly sucked me in. I think I am at a step when I run a bit and freeze. Now I am in limbo. The state is really disgusting. I am neither on the top nor on the bottom. I am nowhere. At the present time, I am in a state of a jump. I jumped, saw something, got a breath of fresh air, but I feel this pull from below which is bringing me down. This pull is very strong today, and I know it is going to bring me down. I understand it is going to happen anyway, and I also understand that I need to jump all the time. I need to jump more frequently. There should be a constant inner training that would lead to a new state.

You will not wake up without a group

— You need to get fixed on the level of the new vibrations you felt. Our task is to get to a higher level of vibrations and not to drop down to sleep again. That's what group is for. Our group is a great opportunity for our spiritual development. You need to understand this. The interaction of people in the group, the process of group formation, strengthening, and development are critically important. I keep repeating it. I am repeating it now for those who have come here for the first time.

The group is a necessary link of our spiritual movement. We get together frequently. You need mirrors. You need to be with people who have the same intention as you. You cannot do this work with people who don't have this intention. They are asleep. If you were to deal with them only, you would fall asleep without being awakened.

— *This happened to me before.*

— I repeat again and again, and I will continue to repeat that without a group you will not be able to wake up. The group should become an organism built on new principals of interactions. The seminars I conduct are jump starts of awareness. In between the seminars, you have to do the group work. You need to constantly work in groups in order to work through, solidify, and fix what happened during the seminar.

If you do this, your chance of moving toward yourself is real. I have conducted many seminars. Different themes of self-investigation were reviewed in details and are being reviewed in different cities. The video and audio recordings of these seminars and webinars where certain aspects of our work are being reviewed in details are available. Buy them and work with them, as I do not intent to repeat myself. This is not an elementary school. Work with the school materials all the time. By doing this, you will receive vibrations of higher frequency that by itself is a necessary prerequisite for you to understand something new in yourself. This is very important, and it should be done by everyone. Please understand the importance of the group; help to create and develop it.

People from different cities participate in our process. People who did not know each other conduct seminars together. For the people who initiate and organize them, it is a privilege. The organizer of a seminar receives a big profit of awareness. Anyone here who has the intention of organizing a seminar can do it. Any offer that coincides with our common intention will be realized. I guarantee that. The opportunities for growth here are tremendous.

Your intention, its strength and realization, depend on you only, but opportunities of its realization here are limitless. Listening to audio recordings will keep you awake and working. The group with whom you interact will allow you to maintain the state of awareness. The seminars you come to and organize will help you to take another step. Those are the opportunities. If you use them, your movement in the direction of yourself would be real. Whether you do it or not depends only on you.

You can talk about the importance of spiritual development, but unless you participate in group work and seminars, you will fall asleep fast. It happens frequently. But then what kind of questions can we discuss? Opportunities here are limitless. You need to use them. I recommend you listen to the recordings of the seminars you attend. You will find that you missed a lot. When you listen to it third time, something new will open up. This is a crucial moment. There is an opportunity to stand up and walk the way to become aware of yourself here. **To stand up on the way means to become aware of your personage as a personage.**

You have entered a higher level of vibrations, and you need to stay there. This will not be easy. It will require you to work through the old programs downloaded into your personality. Those programs will repeat themselves and recur at each level of your movement toward yourself. It's a spiral process. The foundation that was built in childhood is that basic structure from which you would scoop up the necessary material.

Many people come here saying, "When are we going to be done? I want to be enlightened faster." You will not be able to do it faster. For example, it takes a long time to connect the "man—woman" duality. This is not an external connection, when one so-called side looks for another side. Using such an approach, these sides would remain separated. They would remain halves. If you want to become whole, you need to

73

connect these dualities in yourself. You need to explore and to learn both man and woman inside yourself. **Your interactions with the opposite sex show what you do not understand in yourself.** When you start to become aware of this situation, you will be able to change the quality of relationships of your inner man and your inner woman.

You cannot be "simply aware." "I am aware. I am just aware." It does not make sense. What am I aware of? You need to be aware of what happens mechanically, i.e. mechanicality and awareness are two polarities of one duality. There is no awareness without mechanicality. It is impossible. There is nothing to become aware of then.

— *So, in order to be serious, one needs to create a circus, and in order to have serious thoughts one needs to joke around.*

— Who wants to have serious thoughts, and what are serious thoughts? Look, you have two directors. One says, "We need to be very serious." Another one declares, "We need to be very not-serious." But they represent two sides of one coin, like two human beings who are tied together back-to-back, each looking in opposite direction without any understanding of what the other is doing. When you are aware of duality, you see both directors simultaneously. Without awareness, you simply fall into one side of a duality, and at the same time the opposite side pulls you toward itself.

Tie two people together and tell one of them that he needs to reach a certain point that is right in front of his eyes quickly. Tell another man to reach another point that is located in the opposite direction. The first one would run and the second, seeing his aim moving away will also start running. The first one is tired already, but his opponent is dragging him in the opposite direction. Eventually, he gathers his strength. He screams, "Where am I? I was so close to my goal," and starts to push back. They pull and pull on the rope, not moving from the spot from which they started. They spend a lot of energy because their desires are opposite from each other. Until you see how this mechanism is being realized by your personality, you will not be able to manage it.

— *So, in order to wake up one needs to be asleep, and to be aware of the fact that one is dual.*

— Disharmony occurs by falling to one side of a duality. Mechanicality is one side, awareness is another. Mechanicality is what a sleeping one is constantly in. For a sleeper, awareness is just a word that was said by someone. You can repeat it in sleep as a mantra, but that would not lead to anything. Our way leads through the voltage of the spreading of two sides of dualities. In this particular case, we are talking about the duality "mechanicality—awareness," and this voltage may be very high. Actually, it is precisely the high voltage that provides the opportunity to see both sides of duality.

— *Here is my situation. I want to understand what I represent in life. I am a biological creature inside which something died and something new developed. It cannot make sense of anything. It needs to adjust and to look at itself in a new light. People are on a bus with me riding to work, and I project myself onto them. Here is a homeless man lying on the street. Part of me wants to move away from him because he stinks. But another part says, "Stay! Smell it!" I don't like it. I am thinking, "In reality, this being is similar to me. Something inside of me is similarly rotten and smelly. I just had an opportunity to see the physical aspects of it." I hang around, and I smell it.*

— Nobody will give you anything. You have to work. **Everything that happens to you in this life is created by you, but you do not understand it.**

— *This situation caught my attention.*

75

— If something caught your attention, you need to become aware of the duality that was activated by the situation.

— *What should happen in order for me to see it?*

— I repeat, you need to start seeing the specific duality that you have activated. I repeat multiple times, but no one hears it. You keep singing your own songs.

— *In this particular case, the duality is "clean—dirty." Am I correct?*

— Okay. Start to investigate it. Is it "clean—dirty" or something else? What irritates you in this homeless man? Is it the fact that he is without a tie or the fact that he is without a job? Perhaps it's the fact that he is penniless or the fact that he has no place to sleep. What is it exactly? That's what needs to be investigated. You cannot do it all at once. You can find one duality and then suddenly see another. Then, the third one will pop up. You need to pay attention to this.

First, if something irritates you, you need to allow yourself to feel this irritation. That's what we were doing yesterday. To put it simply, that was "love—hate." Love attracts, hate repulses. Hate declares itself differently: irritation, aversion, aggression, wrath, condemnation, hysteric outburst. You can continue yourself. Those are different states that reflect non-acceptance of something. Currently, you understand that non-acceptance, hate in its different forms, appears as a result of one of my sides meeting another side of me.

There is nothing in life except you. If you think someone slipped you a dirty bum in order for you to smell his bad breath, you are mistaken. If you think this bum has nowhere to go but stay in front of your eyes, you are mistaken again. The only correct way to understand

is to understand that everything I encounter in my life is me. Out of all those things, some cause irritation, i.e. hate. Until you accept that you have both love and hate at the same time, you will not be able to perceive them as two sides of one coin.

Can you separate your states

— Begin by separating different states of hate. As we figured out yesterday, you cannot do it. You do not feel the gradations of that state. They are very different, ranging from simple dissatisfaction to aggression, and leading to homicide. Look, we are dealing with different levels of one scale here. You have probably seen situations on TV when someone who was just sitting quietly suddenly picks up a knife and kills another human being. People ask him, "What happened?" He replies, "I don't know. We got drunk, and I killed him." He does not see how the state in which he killed another man developed. He does not know how he moved to the highest level of the state of aggression or to the lowest level of the state of consciousness, to put it differently. He does not understand it.

If you are sensitive, you will initially feel just a touch of a dislike. Then it would transfer to something else. But a human being, especially a spiritually developing human being, says, "We don't have any hate; we love everyone. What kind of hate are you talking about? Those who are not in our group are full of hate, but not us. We are going to enlighten them." And how do they enlighten? They do it aggressively. But they do not see it. It is present in them, but they do not see it. If you don't see it inside of yourself, how can you do anything about it? When I asked you yesterday who do you hate amongst the people here, you replied, "Everything is good and normal. I don't love some of them, but to hate, no…" What is this? It is a total block of awareness of a the state of hate. You do not feel the whole spectrum of your hate state. Please, allow yourself to feel it.

— *A couple years ago, I experienced extreme points of love and hate. I was practically going nuts, and I forbade myself to feel. I blocked myself and became indifferent. Later on, I understood that this was not a solution either. It is a horrific feeling when you become indifferent.*

— To become indifferent means not to feel anything. In such a state, you can kill someone in an instant. Dostoevsky in his novel *Demons* asks a question: "Why does a Russian man sit there praying and suddenly gets up and cuts someone to pieces?" It happens when one is not aware of his hate and one's aggression is released in a flash, as steam from a kettle. One grabs an ax and kills. But prior to that, there were different shades of hate one was not even aware of. And you will not feel these states if you consider them inadmissible. That is how it usually happens. The negative is bad and should not be felt, but then there is no positive either, as negative and positive are two sides of one scale. By deadening one of the sides, you simultaneously deaden the other, opposite side. You should start to investigate this so-called negative side. I repeat that positive and negative are technical terms similar to plus and minus in a car battery. Which one is good in a battery and which one is bad: plus or minus?

— *Neither one is bad.*

— Neither one is bad. But here it appears we have a situation when negative is bad. Allow yourself to imagine, you just killed someone. You all have those thoughts and they pop up all the time, usually for trivial reasons. A man steps on your foot and you explode as if he wanted to kill you. You are ready to kill him. Pay attention to the fact that this happens as a result of him stepping on your foot. What if someone were to point a gun at you? And what if you were to have a gun at the time? What would you do? You would fire. That is what soldiers do, saying that war is the occupation for real men. We need to open that side, but it would not be easy. You need to allow yourself to see these negative states inside of you. You need to allow yourself to see and to feel the entire diapason of these states. For example, you are on a bus and suddenly you feel that you don't like this human being sitting across from you. You allow yourself to feel all the nuances of that state. Suddenly, you see that he irritates you, and later you feel a strong contempt toward him. You feel that if you were to have a gun in your hand, you would have killed him, and if you were to have a knife in your hand, you would have cut him to pieces. These feelings are present in every one of us, but they are blocked.

— *Can I describe what I have just seen? I got into a state of depression, and I had a desire to die. In a flash, without thinking it through, I cut my belly up.*

— Your aggression can be directed outside, prompting you to harm or kill others, or toward yourself, prompting you to harm or kill yourself. In Japan, aggression is commonly expressed the second way—people commit hara-kiri. There is an enormous level of hate that Japanese do not allow themselves to express. They are constantly smiling.

— *I saw my aggression, but in reality, I cannot kill anyone.*

— I remember a book about crimes written during the Soviet era. It was about an average man who was considered to be a good family man and had many friends. One night he was driving with a co-worker in a car. A woman with a sprained ankle signaled them, asking for a lift. They picked her

79

up, drove her to the deserted woods, raped, killed, and burned her. Both men had families. Both were well respected members of a community. Imagine that. What is this? Where did it come from? How can sleeping consciousness explain this? There is a common cause to all these cases: I was drunk. I killed because I was in a state of affect. Another good explanation for the court: he was psychologically abnormal. But who is normal here? There is no such thing as normal here. "Normal" is just a dial position on my washing machine. But such explanations allows him to be sent to a psychiatric ward instead of a jail. That is how twisted everything is here.

— *It will come back anyway. One will have to pay. That is not the best solution.*

— Yes, one will have to pay. Not because God is angry, but because you investigate the experience of both sides of duality. The more you indulge in the experience of one side, the more your experience of the opposite side will be.

— *What if I understand what is happening to me?*

— You do not understand yet. You are just touching the possibility of understanding. Let's not rush. What you have just heard is not what you currently experience. **One has to start to experience one's negative side and to become aware of it.** You cannot even let it out. You say you cannot kill, and I say you can. Under certain circumstances, you will kill people.

— *You mean if there was no fear of punishment?*

— Yes. War, where killing of the enemy is an act of heroism, is a good example of this. We need to see how we do this.

— *In our thoughts ... occasionally ... we all ...*

— We do it not only in our thoughts. Everyone is killing everyone here, and this process does not require a gun. It is not punishable by law. You do not get under a law that would make you a criminal, but you kill. You kill your kids. You kill men and women around you. You kill everything you encounter. You will start to see it. Hate and aggression exist and work independently of your understanding of these states. If you do not see them, they work even more actively.

By observing the negative and the positive in yourself, you will see their interaction. That is the process of self-investigation. When you start to touch it, you will see how you kill. You will start seeing it in the relationship with your relatives. You will start seeing it in the relationship with people you say you love. You will see yourself manifesting hate. It will turn out that the acts you have seen as loving acts are the manifestation of hate. I describe to you what you will encounter following the direction in which we are moving. I am not saying it is easy, it's not. The majority of people do not even admit the presence of all of this in their system, and if you were to tell them they have it, they may kill you.

— *Is cancer a manifestation of killing?*

— Yes.

— *What about suicide?*

— Correct. Aggression goes either outside or inside. Some personalities tend to express aggression externally. They turn into killers. Those who direct aggression inside destroy their own health, destroy themselves. With this understanding, you can see that the real cause of all the diseases you have are the consequences of manifestations of your own hatred toward yourself. You constantly manifest aggression. You are unable to not manifest it, but you do not see it. You manifest this aggression externaly and internaly. These two opposite manifestations of aggression are interconnected. **The**

81

presence of a certain disease should prompt one to start thinking about the reasons for this particular affliction.

By being on the lower levels of three lowest chakras, you activate strong energies of destruction. And the stronger you activate them, the more energy joins you. You release the signal toward which those energies rush. If you hate something strongly, you send that signal. And the essences of those types of energies start to attract to you strongly. In this way, escalation of your internal conflict occurs. Why do killings occur? A couple of friends are playing cards. Suddenly, one of them jumps up. Screaming that the other is cheating, he grabs a knife and kills him. It happens very fast. He is submerged in aggression and hate. These essences surround him and stimulate to manifest the vibrations of the lower quality.

We need to start seeing this. Self-investigation is a vision of dualities of one's own personality when the so-called bad side of oneself denies and projects itself onto other people. By conducting self-investigation, you will start to declassify and to clear your personalities of the mines of dualities. They are similar to the mines that are inserted into the field of low vibrations. Until you touch and clear them, they will stay there, detonating from time to time.

— *At certain moments, I see it in me. I become aware of it, but I do not know what to do.*

— You are in a rush. You jump over. "I see. I am aware. What do I do now?" That's what people commonly say. In reality, you are just approaching the possibility of seeing it. If you were truly to see it, you would not ask, "What do I do with it now?" But you constantly ask me this question. In answering it, I am raising my voice. I do this so you will hear what I say. A soft voice puts you to sleep. So, I have to scream. Perhaps, you will hear something now. That is why I am raising my voice. I do not do it because I am irritated by you. This might be the only way for you to hear something.

How to clear the chakras of the landmines

— When you clear away your next psychological mine, you will say, "I moved forward a little bit." When you clear away your next mine, you will say, "I can see a little bit." You will continue with this process. On the other hand, you can say, "Opa! I see everything. Everything is great. I cleared all the mines. I am enlightened. But, I feel somewhat uneasy. Please, tell me why do I have this funny feeling when I have cleared everything up?" And then you will recall my words: "I just cleared up a little, a very small bit, and the stronger my aspiration toward this process, the stronger I will continue to do it." But don't consider yourself enlightened doing it. By the way, do you understand what enlightenment means?

The clearing of these dual psychological mines will recur on the next levels of consciousness. There are many of these levels, and they are laid out on different levels of every lower chakra. If you cleared it on the lowest levels of the chakra, they will appear later on the higher levels, where their clearing will occur less dramatically. At the same time, it will be much more difficult to see them. So, the higher you go, the more difficult it is to see these psychological mines. By discovering and becoming aware of them, you will receive an external confirmation of this fact, i.e. what you did internally, you will be able to see externally. But in order to see it, you need to be very attentive and vigilant to everything that happens around you. **For example, you suddenly see yourself wanting to kill someone. You become aware of it. Later on, you may** encounter an external situation where an acquaintance of yours was killed or died, and you will recognize or see it.

— *It is somewhat scary, but there is no escape from it.*

— Where can you run from it? Where can you run from your own fear? Until you understand its illusory nature, it is not going to leave you. You are saying, "I have no fear now. If I were to encounter fear, then I would be scared." You are expressing the fear of fear. It's not just fear, it is fear of fear.

— *Everyone here probably just experienced this feeling, fear of fear. I feel I really can kill if my kids or grandkids are threatened. Even though I really try to understand something, I probably would not be able to think straight if something of that nature happens.*

— What does it mean: *"if my kids or grandkids are threatened"*?

— *Well, if someone was about to kill them.*

— Who is your son? Who is your grandson? Do you understand that they are you? You are everywhere—only you. What is it precisely that will excite you to such a degree that you would jump to your guns? We need to investigate this step by step. I repeat again and again, we need to do this hard work to elucidate all the dualities of your personality. You said that if your grandson was threatened, you would kill. Who is your grandson? In reality, we are not talking about your grandson. We are discussing you. What precisely should be threatened in you in order for you to kill?

— *His life is about to be taken away. So, it means my own security.*

— Yes. That is **the lowest of the chakras—security**. Now observe the duality "danger—safety." Start to investigate it.

— *This duality is connected to fear of death?*

— It is connected to the illusion of death. Look, while conducting self-investigation, you will come to the realization that there is no death. A mortal is afraid of death more than anything else because he believes that there is nothing after it. He thinks he will disappear. Those are the notions of the level of consciousness of the lowest obertones of the lower chakras.

— It means that I, insisting that death is just a transformation and telling everyone that I am not afraid of death, in reality project this fear onto my son and grandson. In reality, I am horribly afraid of it.

— Exactly. All these words about immortality and eternal life are just party talk. People say, "There is no death, we are eternal, we are god's creatures," but as soon as someone threatens them, they are ready to kill. Why do they react this way if there is no death? It means, in reality, they do not understand it.

— They fool themselves.

— Yes, we are constantly fooling ourselves.

— The stronger the emotion, the more observant we should be.

— Why do I constantly talk about what is called negative here? I do it because when something so-called positive happens to you, you fall into a deeper sleep. Someone tells you that you are a great spiritual seeker, honorable woman, heavenly mother, etc. Those are lullabies for your ego. A heavenly mother with heavenly kids goes to the zoo to see heavenly animals. Suddenly, someone steps on her foot. Boom! That is precisely the moment you can become aware of your deep sleep. When something is unpleasant and irritating to you, you want to get rid of those feelings as soon as possible. You don't want to get rid of the positive. No, you say, "Tell me more. Tell me how good of a woman I am. Tell me how good of a mother I am."

I, on the other hand, more frequently talk about the negative side of your personality in order to stimulate your awakening. But it is being met with, "He is not a teacher, and even if he is, this is definitely not the teaching of light. He is some kind of a demon; let's get out of here." And it happens because I don't rub your ego the way it likes to be rubbed. I start with the side that needs to be worked on in order to awaken you. I am not trying to put you to sleep; quite the opposite, I am constantly waking you up.

You have to start working with what you do not like. It is precisely through what you don't like that your consciousness can be activated. Use this side of duality to strengthen awareness. Never consider your awareness to be full, as even when you come to what is considered to be full awareness here, you will suddenly find yourself on the very first step of another level of being, where you will feel like a child. By ascending to the highest level of that plane, you will get to the next level, where you will be a child again.

So, let us drop these conversations about who is the most enlightened here. Always use awareness, since without it, it is impossible to move toward your true self. **The more negative will you see in the positive and positive in the negative, the deeper will your awareness be.**

What I discuss now we can call a prelude. It is a warm up to stimulate you to do it. Later we will have specific discussions on how you do it and what you get out of it. **You are irritated by something in someone. You start to investigate what it is that irritates you. Remember, what irritates you is in you. It is not in him. It is not in her. But you see it in him or her.** What exactly irritates you? Let's investigate.

— *Why is one afraid to admit to himself that he can hate someone? Is it because one is afraid of himself?*

86

— Fear is generated by the essences that feed on fear. These essences are present on the three lowest chakras, and they use human beings for their nourishment. They need the vibrations of fear. They feed on them. You are a restaurant for them. They need to be fed well, and the restaurant starts to work hard. For example, a good daily return from such a restaurant can be provided by scary things we constantly hear and see on TV. Take a look at any daily news program. What is constantly being discussed is that something was blown away, someone was killed or raped, a terrorist act was committed somewhere. Is not this a stimulation of fear? And the restaurant is working at full speed. That is why I repeat: this is fear of fear. It is fear squared. Essences that eat at your restaurant of fear are not interested in their food being taken away. It does not mean they are bad. They just feed on fear. They get their own experience here. Jackals feed on cadaveric meat. It does not mean jackals are bad. This is just what they eat.

So, what is the quality of food in your restaurant? Who are you going to feed there? What are you going to serve there? Don't forget, we ourselves feed on vegetable and animal food, but someone also feeds on us. The question is who do you choose to feed? Nobody asks a sleeper to answer this question. He is just a bistro called "Fear." However, in the process of waking up, you begin to understand that you can entertain other guests that require food of completely different qualities of vibrations. They feed on high vibrations of what we can call Unconditional Love. Are you capable of generating that kind of food? Your ability to transform the food you take in—vegetable, animal, air and impressions—into a higher vibration food is the basic parameter of your so-called spiritual advancement.

When, as a result of the transformation of the so-called here "love—hate," you start to produce Unconditional Love; you transform into a restaurant for Powers of Light. You start to produce different food. By becoming more and more enlightened, you attract them more. I am using analogies that show how things are now and how they will change.

The main aim of the training ground "Earth" is to exit the influences that give birth to fear. Generally speaking, the whole cosmos represents one big training ground. Our process is training inside training. It never ends. The aim of the training Earth is the combination, synthesis, and integration of the dualities of the personal structure of a human being.

— *Are we here in order to move to another playground?*

Joining dualities and chakras

— We are here to assimilate all the lessons of the training ground "Solar System." For the majority of people it is a distant aim. Nevertheless, this is a real aim that one needs to keep in mind. Take a look at how the movement toward oneself occurs as related to chakras. Let's take, for example, the first seven chakras, each one consisting of twelve obertones. You can say that a certain chakra of yours is open, but which of its obertones are open? Which obertone did you get to? Were you able to establish yourself there?

— *What is an obertone?*

— Every chakra is a certain diapason of vibrations. The diapason that a certain chakra encompasses can be divided into twelve obertones or sub-levels, and each one of which then can be divided into another twelve, etc.

— *I sense aggression arising to what you are saying.*

— Your mind is getting screwed up. Excellent. I say concrete things but always with a certain degree of relativity. So, try to relate to this not as to the Truth with a capital "T," but as working concepts that will allow you to better understand our work. I am going to continue despite your aggression. The synthesis of opposite qualities proceeds through the interaction of two neighboring chakras. I already discussed two Godly Qualities manifested in the training "Earth." Those are Will of the Mind and Love—Wisdom. The first chakra is Will of the Mind. The second chakra, svadhistana is Love—Wisdom. The level of vibrations of those chakras is low. The majority of people are on the level of vibrations of those two chakras. If you happen to be on the lowest levels of the first chakra obertones, you would only be capable of killing other people while fighting for survival. What would you do if you happen to be on the lowest levels of svidhastana?

— *Rape?*

— You would screw everything that moves, and you would do it without love. You would do it as an animal. That is the level of a male and female animal. When you move toward mastering the third chakra, muladhara, and the fourth chakra, anahata, you start to transfer to the higher levels of vibrations. Joining of the third and the fourth chakras on the highest levels of their obertones provides an opportunity to feel what is called Godly Love here. That is the work of the highest emotional center. The joining of the fifth and the sixth chakras provides an opportunity to enter the highest intellectual center. The joining of the energies of all those chakras on the level of seventh chakra, sahasrara, starts the initiation of transformation of your consciousness, and you start seeing what happens outside the Earth. You become aware of yourself as a Multilevel Consciousness. You start to understand that your personality represents just a fragment of who you really are. You start to experience and understand yourself on multiple levels. In order to get to this point, you need to complete the work of joining dualities, i.e. the opposite energies that are present in every human being.

I want to say couple of words regarding exits into astral. Even if you were to exit into astral, you would only get to the levels that correspond to the levels of vibration of your consciousness. If your consciousness happens to be on the level of the three lowest chakras, you would simply wander around the astral planes of the lowest vibrations.

— *Well, it can be used as an indicator of where you currently are.*

— But in order to use it as an indicator, you should understand where you are. In order to understand where you are, you need to see it from the higher vibrations of consciousness.

— *Even in astral?*

— Especially in astral. I invite you to feel what we just discussed. Does anyone want to share your resonance to our conversation? Please do so. We need to spin it to the fullest. A certain resonance occurs between you and these vibrations. It leads to you taking a certain idea that resonated with you and investigating it. You will find out that everything I discuss is interconnected. One has to start somewhere and slowly collect the whole picture. Tell us what resonated with you.

— *What resonated strongly with me was this reciprocal killing you discussed and our complete lack of awareness of harming others, our inability to see it, and our fear. I was told that my thoughts hurt others, but I am unable to see the mechanism of it. I am afraid to think badly about others. In order not to do it, I prefer not to think at all.*

90

— And not to feel. This is what resonated with you now; therefore, this is very important for you. You are ready to start to investigate and to see this.

What can you start self-investigation with? Take any given human being and start to examine your projections onto him or her. Then take another one and start the same process again. Your projections need to be spoken out aloud with an understanding that those are your projections. That is why I am saying that you cannot do this work alone. There should be a stimulus and our group provides this stimulus.

When you get together as a group, you will always have a theme, and you will always find another member with whom to discuss it. It may be more than one member and more than one theme. It may be few themes with different people or few themes with one member. You always have what to be aware of and what to discuss. It should not be a casual conversation accompanied by a cup of tea, but a discussion of your awareness. It is not easy to find people who will discuss this. We created a certain atmosphere here and people are not gathered here coincidentally. Moscow is a big city, and we have only a handful of people here. Are you ready to use this opportunity?

— *Yes.*

— Excellent. You start to explore a certain theme, and it will lead to the next vision. I gave you a boost. You accepted it and started to spin it. I am not here to tell you everything. I am here to give you a kick start, but you need to develop it on your own. Other kicks will follow as we go along. They will ignite more inner work. Doing this work you will understand more and more of what exactly you are doing, and nobody will be able to take it away from you. It will be yours, and what is yours you can pass on to others who are asleep. It is impossible to talk about awareness with those who are in deep sleep, but you will have to interact with them anyway. You will have no choice, but you will know how to do it. With those who are ready to wake up, it will happen differently. There will be many different nuances.

— Can I say something? When I relaxed a few minutes ago, I understood that I would look at my actions and tell others what is going on. I received a mental picture of me standing inside a store checking out a costume for a child. I realize I want to buy it as a gift and try to figure out why am I doing it. And suddenly the understanding came that I can exhaust people, especially people who are close to me with my attention and caring attitude toward them. On the other hand, I might be doing it to elevate myself: "Be grateful to me for what I did for you."

— You start seeing different methods of your own manipulations. We buy something for a child, but why? Yes, we want to do something pleasant for a child, but at the same time we want a child to depend on us, in order for us to reprimand him later on. Every act has two opposite sides. One needs to see both of them. When you see both of them, they start to transform.

— When I saw it, I felt a curtain lowered. I started to see better. Using this example, I understand how to look and what to look for.

— Exactly. You will see many similar examples. You will see it on a daily basis, in your every action.

— I saw a man walking. I saw different essences in different parts of his body. These essences were corresponding to different sounds. I perceived this picture as his walk of life. He was walking and feeling these vibrations. He was choosing the way to walk in order to resonate with these essences. By avoiding the resonance with the essences of the level of consciousness of the lower vibrations, he was balancing his state. He was illuminating his way.

92

When you start to experience gratitude for the old experience, you take a step toward something new

— When you offer your body, i.e. the house you temporarily occupy, to the essences of higher and higher vibrations, your life changes completely. But it does not mean that you need to throw the old tenants out. If you do that, they would feed off you even more. Simply thank them and let them go. Remember how a first grader finishes first grade. He thanks his teachers and moves on.

He does not curse his teachers. He thanks them. They are not bad. They are the way they are. However, if you don't need to have the experience connected to them any longer, you express gratitude for the experience you have lived through with them, and you move on to the experience of the next quality.

— *So, this is the sensation I need to be aware of while making every step. Every step may take me back to where these essences of the lower vibrations rule.*

— You need to see the shows in which they participate. Until you see them, you cannot let go of anything. People scream, "Free yourself. Clean yourself up. Let it go." What do you have to clean yourself from? What do you have to let go of? It is not clear.

By investigating these shows thoroughly, you can come to understand them. If you really understand what you lived through and experienced, express your gratitude and move on to a higher energy level of a given chakra, or to the next chakra, occupied by the essences of higher vibrations. This move will provide you with another experience, of which you will also need to become aware.

So, separation from something or letting something go, in reality, is the addition or integration that occurs through the holistic vision of what you have lived through. Therefore, **the basic question is who am I now, and who can I become later on?** Later will happen later. Later is the opening of the next levels. Now is now. It is neither bad nor good, but if you want to move forward, you need to see clearly what is happening now.

— But the present builds on the past. One probably would need to return to the past.

— In your present, everything is past. Only in the illusion of linear time does it appear that the past has passed and we forgot it. No, every single moment of the present carries every second of the past in it. All our thoughts, feelings, and actions result from what happened in the past. We carry it along. A little girl who was scorned and a little boy who was hurt are always inside. They will not disappear until you review all the painful experiences of your past. They will not disappear until this boy and girl receive what they needed to receive back then.

We can change our future only by changing our past. Otherwise, we would constantly recreate our past in our future, i.e. repeat it. The point of the intersection of the past and the future is the current moment. It is through the current moment that we can change our fate, as it belongs to both our past and our future. But in order to do so, one has to become aware of oneself in the past coming from the notions of oneself in the future. Most people think that the past is something that happened and cannot be changed. This is not so.

— *So, if I return to the situation I lived through and replay it, review it from a new point of view ... fill it with new feelings and emotions...*

— What you lived through back then is just one of the options of living through a situation. You return, and you experience it differently. The whole experience of your life can be viewed as a collection of Lego pieces that you can put together differently. This is your own construct that you worked up yourself. Now you can put these pieces together any way you want and receive completely different configurations of your experience. In this way, by changing the past, you change the future, and by changing the future, you change the past. You begin to understand that past and future represent a certain illusion of a given training playground and start to create your life in full awareness.

The training playground "Earth" was created in order to prepare human consciousness for creativity of higher levels. On a current level, creativity has only physical characteristics. We embody our thoughts and feelings into physical objects and situations. This is a peculiarity of creativity of the three-dimensional reality. All your thoughts and feelings always lead to something physical. This illusion is created by your mind. By changing your mind, you can change your surroundings, similarly to kids playing in a sandbox. They build something out of sand, and then they break it to build something new. But this game has a major limitation that I call duality. While being present in duality, you can only create contradictions. That is why exiting duality is so

important for us. That is the only way to start to create from intention, not from the opposite desires.

— I have impressions from childhood. I remember my kindergarten, certain pictures. Someone hurt me there really bad. I am constantly trying to figure out who it was. I want to return and replay this situation, but as soon as I see that kindergarten room or smell kasha, I get nauseated. What is it?

— In order to understand this, one needs to review and rescreen old shows of one's life. It is precisely through those reviews that you can enter these situations and change them. During an individual review, you can exit this reality and enter other realities. You can solve what appears to be unsolvable here.

— So, it is possible?

— Yes.

— Initially, I had an impression of a total chaos, but now, after you said what you have said, I see a picture. If now we create the future, we have to sincerely see what we are in right now. One cannot move forward by building the illusions and fooling oneself. I just saw what kind of a mess is in my head. One can only build a new playground if one honestly acknowledges to himself, irrespective of how painful and scary it is, what one is currently in.

— Exactly. Also, remember that you will not be able to understand everything we discuss right away. It will happen gradually. So, buy the audio and video materials of our school and work with them. By listening to them, you will extract certain moments with which you will resonate at that moment and spin it to awareness. And the more you review, spin, and become aware, the bigger and more voluminous your vision will be.

— I realize that aggression and hate are constantly present in a human being. It is quite high based on what we have seen yesterday. It is

just waiting to be expressed. Everyone carries and reacts to his own set of hooks. And one will inevitably spill it out. The reaction can be stronger or weaker depending on the situation.

— Yes, that happens constantly, either externally or internally.

— *So, there is certain level of aggression that needs to be spilled somehow. It is just waiting for a cause.*

— Well, the cause will always be found by the conditioned mind.

— A man is drinking. He is asked, "Why do you drink?" "How can one not drink here?" he answers.

— *That is right.*

— One starts shooting. And how can one not shoot if everyone around here wants to kill me? Behind all of this is hate. This hate simply finds different forms of expression and different explanations.

— *I am trying to figure out what we can do about it.*

— Nothing. We need to see it clearly. There is nothing to do. You start right away: "Oh! Horror! What can I do?" You have lived in this all your life, and now, seeing just a tiny part of it, you get hysterical. What did you do before? Begin to see what you are in, just observe. Awareness is action. It changes the program of the old matrix of consciousness. One does not need to grab a shovel and start to do something. One sees something and immediately starts to think what to do with it. Should I move it away? Should I sell it? Should I throw it away? No. To see means to see your persona the way it is right now. Yes, there is a lot of hate there. Yes, that is the way you are. When you start to see it, it will start to change. The holistic vision itself changes everything. Nothing else needs to be done.

— I thought it had to be balanced by some physical action. I thought one had to hit a pillow or something.

One can hit a pillow or one can become aware of why one is hitting a pillow

— Hit a pillow or spit on someone outside. If that is not enough, tell a cop that you despise our legal system and him personally. Tell him you do not have a passport, show him a gun, and threaten to shoot him. Then you will experience a turn of events. That's the way to end up in jail. In jail, you will release steam differently. That is precisely how it happens, but it happens mechanically. We need to be aware. One may hit a pillow or become aware of why one is hitting a pillow.

— What if I were to hit a pillow with awareness?

— Being aware, you will not hit a pillow.

— Aggression typically looks for a physical action.

— Okay. Hit a pillow. Kill it. Burry it. Cry over it. Do what you have to do, but do it with awareness. I warn you. You have a tendency to act physically. By doing it, you can simply release some steam and continue to remain in your usual, sleepy state of consciousness. You will simply release the oversupply of aggression while remaining asleep. **In order to create a situation of awareness, one needs to do something one is not in a habit of doing.** You want to hit a pillow?! Don't do it. Lie down and become aware of the reason you desire to hit a pillow. Become aware of it. If you simply hit and tear up the pillow, you will not have a reason to become aware of why you did it. And for the one who is not in the habit of hitting pillows, perhaps it is necessary to hit

98

one. One needs to do something one is not accustomed of doing. That will lead to an opportunity to become aware.

— *To go against one's habit.*

— Yes. It is precisely by doing what you are not accustomed to doing that you create an opportunity for awareness, since what you are used to doing keeps you asleep.

— *One has to brake some dishes.*

— One can break some dishes, but one can also wash some dishes. For example, you can start washing dishes for people you do not even know. Knock on someone's door and say, "Let me wash your dishes."

— *There is an old saying: a couple times a day you should do something you have never done before or do everything differently. You will receive a new experience.*

— But don't do it just to do something differently. Do it for awareness. It will stimulate awareness.

— *True. Some kind of a mechanism is working. Suddenly, I understand that I will do it again now. I say, "Let me do it differently," and something changes.*

I remember a state from my childhood, a state I felt with my grandmother, a state of tenderness. I remember a state I felt with my parents. These states are completely opposite now. I feel that I experience more tenderness toward my grandmother than she does toward me. From my father comes a state of oppression, and I return the same state to him. I sense that my mother does not even see me, and I cannot see her presence in my life now. I almost never notice her when I am at home.

— I suggesst you break into pairs and discuss what irritates you in others. This will help you to see your own dualities, the activation of which causes you to become irritated. **I remind you that we are dealing with our own parts. It is the parts that we do not see and do not accept in ourselves that irritate us in others**. You need to define them. Our work involves the mind and feelings. You cannot do it based on your feelings alone or only intellectually. You need to learn to feel and to think differently.

Our process is geared toward the development of our emotional and mental bodies. After the so-called physical death, your physical body will be dropped. Our physical body is just a space suit. Instead of the physical body, you will receive an astrosom of the level of vibrations you achieved during your life in a physical body. You will occupy the worlds that will correspond to the vibrations of your astrosom. If you were a religious leader who frightened everyone with hell, you worked up such an astral-mental form which will lead you to that hell. There is infinite number of worlds. The thoughts and feelings that crystalized during your mental and emotional activities will direct you to the corresponding world.

If you sense yourself as a multilevel essence whose seventh and eighth chakras are open, the place you will get to will be very different from the place you will get if you occupy the low vibrations of the first three chakras. This is not God's punishment or the devil's games. No. You create your future yourself by concentrating on the lowest vibrations of your consciousness. Your predominant thoughts and feelings form a quality of vibrations of your astrosom in accordance to which you, after the so-called death, will get to a certain world. It is a consistent pattern.

— *Are there other options to get the work done? Can one come to Earth again?*

— Yes. If you are in rough material vibrations, you will be attracted by the reality of this plane. You will enter it again. It will happen again and again until you exit to the level of the next quality of vibrations of your emotional and mental bodies. This is not revenge but a result of experiences accumulated by your personality. What it worked up, it shall receive. This is how it is. But for now, please, investigate and thoroughly take apart a duality that irritates you.

— *Can I? I was sitting here for two days quietly not knowing what to say, as I understood neither the direction of the work nor the problem on which I wanted to work. And now I understand that the question that brought me in and the thoughts I had while reading your books are not what I want to begin with. I started reading your book when I was diagnosed with cancer. Yesterday, I realized I want to work on a different theme. Yesterday, when we worked in pairs, I had an opportunity to see the girls from the back, and I understood I saw both men and women. I looked at Alla and realized I was seeing a man. Then, I turned my attention to Ludmila sitting on Oleg's laps, and I saw a mother and a child. Those are different roles. At that moment, I did not know what I wanted. If these are all my parts, if there is an opportunity for such a nonjudgmental screen, then why doesn't it show me anything? It is because I do not show myself.* **In observing these situations, I thought, "What do I want from a man? What kind of roles do I assign to him?" I understood that I usually expect him to play certain roles. I either want him to be a friend and to lead deep soulful conversations with him expecting him to offer the same thing in return, or I just have sex with him, morning comes—good bye. I can also play a mother or expect care from him. This is what usually happens. I thought about my inner woman and my inner man, and I asked myself, "Do I want to see my inner man and my inner woman?" Afeter asking myself this question, I fell asleep, and I saw a dream. I saw a man. I did not like his appearance. I thought to myself, "I don't need someone like him." However, he was very kind but did not pay any attention to me as a woman. This was a representative situation. It was set up in some restroom where there was**

101

a clear cut separation on men and women, and where men did not react to me even though we were in the same room. And I understood that I was not a woman for my man. I recall the major problem I had during my marriage. I was married for a few years, and my major problem was that my husband did not perceive me as a woman. I woke up with an understanding that those are precisely the men I meet. Why do I meet those men? It would be interesting to see my inner woman. I said I wanted to see my inner woman, and I fell asleep again. I saw a dream again, woke up, analyzed it, and came to the conclusion that she is neither meat nor fish. I fell asleep again, and when I awoke I had a feeling that everything was erased. I thought that some bad essences did not want me to know my woman. Then I thought, "This is actually simple. In reality, I don't want to know her or I don't want to let her come outside, to reveal her."

— I don't want to bring her to the level of consciousness. In reality, she exists. There is always a man and a woman inside. The first thing you need to understand is that if you have a body of a woman, it does not mean you are only a woman. You are both a man and a woman. If you have a body of a man, you are still a woman and a man. You need to see this clearly. Secondly, you need to start seeing the vibrations that those two internal personages of yours are in. If your consciousness is of low vibrations, there will be conflicts between them. They will be at war. This is related to any duality, but the duality "man—woman" is expressed in the physical bodies and is being discussed more frequently.

A woman is looking for a man, and a man is looking for a woman. In reality, a man and a woman represent two sides of one duality that is present in every human being. The relationship between them is determined by the level of their awareness. If there is no awareness, the war will go on until total annihilation.

— *Are we discussing the external man and woman?*

— **No. We always discuss the internal here.** The external always mirrors the internal. What do you need a man for? Who do you identify with: a man or a woman? Why does homosexuality exist? This is quite simple. One human being in a pair is conscious of himself as a man, while another is conscious of himself as a woman. What is lesbos? It is the same thing. In one woman a male part is being declared, in another—female. Physical bodies do not mean much when you look at them from this point of view.

What determines the scenario of a relationship between a man and a woman? It is determined by the interaction of this pair inside a human being, as externally you attract whatever is inside you. A man who appears in your life reflects your inner man, and a woman who appears in your life reflects your inner woman. Misunderstandings, fights, and wars between them reflect the level of your consciousness. At the levels of consciousness that we call "sleep," nothing else can happen. On the lowest levels of consciousness, that is the only way.

Living with one, to see many in him

— One more thing. **What is a man and what is a woman? What are the roles this duality experiences here in human society? If it is a man, it is father, husband, lover, son, or brother. If it is a woman, it is mother, wife, lover, daughter, or sister. Which one of these roles are you playing now?**

— *Recently, I broke off a very good relationship with a man. I understand now that I broke it off because I predetermined the roles. I told him I was only going to do business with him. But he had many other things to offer. He could have been a friend or a lover. He was against any kind of choices and scenarios. I was not satisfied with that. I understand. I was afraid.*

— What exactly did not satisfy you? Which role did not satisfy you?

— *I was satisfied with each role separately.*

— So, you need to have a collection of men for different relationships.

— *That is how I played it before.*

— Usually that's how it is. In order to experience dualities on the low levels of consciousness, several people are chosen. One is a lover you cannot even talk to, but you feel great in bed with him. Another brings money home, but you don't want to touch him in bed. Another is a son you need to take care of or brother you can discuss everything with.

— *Yes. When I met a real human being who I could talk to and play with, who was bringing money home, and who was great in bed, I got scared and I said, "No."*

— When your partner is capable of playing different roles, you also need to learn to change roles fast. This is not easy. It requires you to change your own images fast. Previously, you discussed a firm and stable perception of yourself. This is what sleeping people like so much. They need everything to remain stable and steady. Every single human being with whom a sleeper comes in contact should have a sharp, definitive image. If he brings money, he should bring money. He should not flirt. I do not need that, because I would have to change my perception of him, and that is quite difficult. I do not need that. My dream is very straightforward. Let's not muddy it.

This situation shows the inflexibility of your perception, your inability to change your own images of yourself. When you master different roles and images of yourself, you can relate to another human being from the point of view of any one of them. For example, you cannot pass through certain situations while being in a role of a lover. Let's say you discovered that your man sleeps with another woman. How would you relate to her as a lover?

— *I will say that I do not care.*

— What does it mean, "I don't care"?

— *I do not feel anything.*

— What exactly don't you feel?

— *I do not feel jealousy.*

— If you do not feel the pangs of jealousy, it does not mean you do not care. You can feel something completely different, unconditional love for example. You can work through and pass through certain situations with a given human being only by changing your image or by transferring into another role. You can accept him having a lover, entering, for example, a mother role and relating to him as you would relate to a son. You can talk to him about the situation out of that role. But if you do not know what mother is, you cannot move to that role. You would create jealousy scenes. On the other hand, you may decide to become a mother. Then you will need a man only to conceive a child. You will have a child with whom you will experience the role of a mother, not needing him as a father.

— *And what if a woman is neither...?*

— What does "neither woman" mean?

— *I am undeclared or sexless. I get up in the morning, come to a mirror, and understand that I do not know who I am.*

— And who here understands who he is here? That is the only sane thought that can come to your head in the morning: "Who am I? I don't understand." You are the one who can play different roles. You have a certain predetermined set of roles. If you do not feel yourself to be a woman right now, it does not mean you do not exist. A TV set is here, even though no program is currently running. If you turn it to CNN channel, it will show CNN. If you turn it to FOX, it will show FOX. The fact that it has not been turned on yet does not mean it does not exist.

— *How can one turn oneself on? One has been sleeping for so long. .*

— In order to turn oneself on, one needs to know what and how to turn on. In order to do that, one needs to figure out the entire set of one's role programs. Currently, we are sorting out the relationship between a man and a woman. As we can see, they can play at least six program roles. In which of those programs do you have experience?

— *I think I am experienced in the mother and daughter roles.*

— So, you have the experience of a daughter. It is impossible not to have it for you. But do you have the experience of being a mother?

— *I think I do.*

— Do you have a child?

— *No.*

— Therefore, you only have the experience that was received from your own mother. Factually, you have the experience of daughter, but you don't have the experience of mother. With the birth of your own child, you start to accumulate the experience of mother. Do you have the experience of a lover?

— *Yes, of course.*

— Do you have the experience of being a wife?

— *Yes.*

— Now we need to look into this experience deeper. What kind of an experience is it? What kinds of dualities were activated by this experience? What are the scenarios of these roles? There might not be enough experience there. Then you will have to look for what is missing. What kind of experience do you want to receive now?

— *It appears to me that we are missing some roles on our list.*

— Which roles are they?

— *How would we see a businesswoman here?*

— This role is connected to work. Businesswoman is a woman that does business. Mother, daughter, son do not do business.

— *Work is not only about money; some people may be quite creative at work. Creativity of one's work is not connected to the duality "man—woman." It is connected to other dualities: "creativity—mechanicality," "rich—poor," if it is business.*

— We have to sort this out very carefully. We want simplicity. Please, let's be as simple and clear as we possibly can. A human being is quite a complex construct, and when one says "i," we have no idea who is talking. A human being is a plural structure, but he does not consider himself to be such, because he identifies with that "i," that particular role he currently plays.

We are receiving experiences of a different kind here. These experiences are connected to dualities. Any given experience of yours is connected to a certain duality or dualities in which you accumulate it. Therefore, in order to understand your experience, you need to see these dualities. And in order to discern what kind of duality with which you are dealing, you need to have a well-developed intellect and open sphere of feelings. The mind and the heart are interconnected, and it is impossible to walk just one line here. The mind and the heart should walk together.

— *What kind of a role does a businesswoman fit into? Is she a mother, a daughter, a wife, or a lover?*

— A businesswoman fits into a role of a "businesswoman." Why do you want to connect a lover and a businesswoman? A lover only receives sexual satisfaction.

— *But businesswoman can also receive sexual satisfaction.*

— Then she is not a businesswoman, but a lover. A prostitute, for example, uses sex in order to make money. This is an example of a businesswoman from sex. Usually she does not experience any sexual pleasure with a client. You cannot experience the pleasure of sex when you want to receive money. At one point, you will meet someone who would give you such pleasure, but he will make you pay for it.

— *Sexual pleasure can be the consequence of love. What if she is getting pleasure out of love?*

— What is love?

— *I mean love the way we understand it, love between a man and a woman.*

— What is love the way we understand it? Everyone understands it differently.

— *In traditional societies a woman uses sex to receive money. She practices prostitution. Her motivation is money. Is it possible to have a different motivation during sex, to receive pleasure? At the same time a different desire, a desire to experience friendship, may be present there. One does not exclude another.*

— That is not simple.

— *I am trying to figure it out.*

Do you understand the differences between the roles you are playing?

— In order to sort it out, you need to have a plan. You say, "It is good to have a friend and on top of it to have sex with him, and it would be great to get some money out of it too." Everything is thrown into one pile, a huge garbage bin full of garbage, and we are trying to figure out what is what there. This can be called by one word only—garbage. But when you start to take it apart, you can see pieces of paper, apples, some dirty hair—many different things that are collectively called "garbage." That is how we talk. In order to sort out what we have, we need to start to discern it first. We need to separate one thing from another, and the more detailed your separation is, the clearer your picture will be.

By participating in a drama that is called "Life" here, a human being plays different roles: mother, father, son, daughter, businessman, member of a chess club, garbage collector, doctor, etc. The roles we are reviewing are present in every culture, but there are other roles that differ in different cultures. In playing all these roles, one acquires a certain experience. When one needs to experience a unique role, one enters the specific culture that offers it. If you need to experience a role of a shaman, you will enter the culture that offers it. What other exotic roles are there?

— *Napoleon.*

— Napoleon is not a role. It is a last name. Last and first names represent certain codes, by the way. In three dimensional reality, such a code determines the scenario of one's life. Medications, for example, have certain names. These are also the codes. You don't have to take medicine.

You can use its code and experience the same effect, albeit without side effects that its physical application may have. The name of a human being is also a code.

— *What happens when one changes one's name? Does the scenario also change?*

— Yes, but the earthly name caries a code of separation. If you were to know your higher name, you would orient toward completely different vibrations. The roles played by us also represent a system of certain codes. By entering these roles, you start to receive something that lies beyond the system of those codes. What kind of roles do you take part in?

— *A role of a good father.*

— "Good" is a characteristic of a role.

— *A role of a worker. A role of a passenger. A role of a pedestrian.*

— Family roles, work roles, roles on vacation, a role of a so-called spiritual seeker. All of these roles provide an opportunity to acquire certain experience. And what is the experience itself connected to? What does it mean to live through it, to experience?

— *It is connected to the feelings one experiences while living through certain situations.*

— Can you just experience feelings?

— *We experience both feelings and thoughts.*

— Okay. Let's say you turn on music. Music can be different. You are sitting at home listening to it. Do you acquire a certain experience?

— *Some kind of a duality should be activated. Then the feelings connected to the activation of a particular duality will be experienced as one lives through the necessary experience.*

— Experience presupposes a certain knowledge and living through this knowledge on the level of feelings.

— *Can we say that this is the opening of the internal space?*

— We can say a lot, but why do you want to call it so?

— *When one experiences something, one's worldview, one's internal universe changes.*

— Everyone has certain expressions they use when he or she tries to say something, but to say something does not mean to understand it. You are trying to introduce what I say into a certain system of notions you have. This is your way of integrating what I pass on to you. That is why I am not going to tell you whether you understand what I say correctly or not. You need to come to this understanding yourself. But I can assure you that what I tell you will change your system of notions about yourself and life in general. Right now the internal adaptation process to what I discuss occurs within you.

So, in executing these roles, we receive a certain experience. In what way do we receive it? **Experience is knowledge acquired by living through a certain situation.** For example, you are asked, "Who are you?" You reply, "I am a Soul. I am a Spirit. I am a cosmic mind." What does this mean? Most likely, this is something you have read. But it does not mean you experienced it. To experience yourself as a multidimensional essence means to have an experience of yourself in different realities. Such an experience entails serious changes of the old, habitual notions you had about yourself.

Why are people able to interact? They interact strangely, but they interact. One says, "I got drunk yesterday." Another replies, "I understand you; I also got drunk yesterday." "What did you drink?" And they discuss who drunk what and what level of drunkenness each one of them got to. They have a certain common experience.

— They have a common system of coordinates where something overlaps.

— They share common labels: labels of drinks they tried or drugs they used. They also have a common experience. You want to talk to an alcoholic? Get drunk and you would have something to talk about. But there is also experience which happens to be very little known. In particular, what I discuss here is experience that does not have significant promulgation here. In order to enter this experience, you need to incorporate a qualitatively different system of notions about yourself.

That system of notions is what we discuss here. Moreover, it requires you to become fully aware of the old system of notions that gave birth to the experience you already have. In order to become aware of the experience you already have, you need to see how you gave birth to it. But there is a certain experience that has not been received yet, or it is in a state of being received. For example, the experience of interaction between a man and a woman. What kind of experience of interaction between a man and a woman do you have?

— Extensive and dramatic experience.

— On what kind of scenario were your interactions based? If you were to become aware of it, you would see that it was based on the same scenario.

— The same scenario. One falls in love, gets enchanted and attracted, and then the war of personalities begins. That is the scenario.

— Yes, and it recurs and recurs. And you have this experience in huge quantities. Every succeeding partner provides you with an opportunity to strengthen it further. Is that so?

— That is so.

— Is there anything new there?

— *Unless one changes, nothing will change.*

— Exactly. The life of a human being in the old matrix of consciousness is a repetition of the same dramatic experience over and over again. The majority of people hope their next experience will be better than the last one. If you were to ask a man *how* he expects his next experience to be, he would provide you with a couple of typical hallucinations. After receiving the next portion of experience he would say, "I thought it would be better, but it turned out to be the usual."

So, the experience that the majority of people acquire is a constant repetition of the same experience. Breaking into something new is a miracle. People live expecting that some changes for the better will occur in their life. Getting older, they understand that nothing better will happen, things will only get worst.

— *They say the opposite. Things were good before. I loved him before.*

— **This is a nostalgia for that first experience that, chewed upon for many years, turned to an old, flavorless bubble gum. It is fun to chew a piece of gum in the beginning, but then it becomes soft and tasteless. You have to spit it out. Nostalgia is a memory of the first, pleasant taste sensations of a new gum. People get together and tell stories. I had such a tasty gum. It used to dissolve in my mouth. Another one cries, saying he had a similar experience. He had strawberry gum, and he loved it very much. Another one recalls having raspberry gum.**

Transfer to the qualitatively new experience is possible only when full awareness of the experience of old quality has been reached. In order to become aware of the old experience you have to take full responsibility for it. **You have to see** that everything that happened and is happening in your life is your own creation.

— *And to write a different script.*

The old scenario of a new life

— What are you going to write in the new scenario?

— *Well, one's notions change.*

— I am not sure they change in the one who is asleep. I just told you that the majority of people come to Earth and live the same scenario, stages of which we reviewed, until death. What other scenario are you talking about? Sit down, get a piece of paper, and write down another scenario. Please, do it. Unless you become totally aware of your old experience, you will simply write the variations of your old scenario, spicing it with the illusion of novelty. It is similar to a TV commercial, the same Snickers but in a different package. Every single time, they change a package; they call it a new Snickers. Is it new? No, it is the old Snickers. If it was to change, it would have a different name, a different code. A Snickers is a Snickers, and nothing you can do about it. So, try to write a new scenario for your life. Most likely, you will do what advertisement agencies do in trying to sell a product. They create an illusion of novelty, and because the majority of people react to the illusions, these advertisements work. So, try to write a new scenario right now. What do you have?

— *Well, more money.*

— That's old.

— *Yesterday was my son's birthday. I came home and nobody was there. There was a vase with flowers in my room. I have three kids, and my husband always brings me flowers on kids' birthdays. His portrait is on a wall, flowers are on a table, and nobody is there. Of course, I experienced nostalgia for the "gum." I grabbed the flowers and started to cry. I have never cried in my life like this. I allowed myself to cry. I was simply nostalgic. Later, this crying turned into blame and pity. What does this mean? I have been coming to your seminars for two years already, but everything is the same: horrific loneliness. I am all alone. I started hitting the walls. I displayed real anger. I displayed wrath.*

— On the lower vibrational levels, a man and a woman fight to death. Unless you see it, you will continue to repeat it.

— *I experienced it to the fullest.*

— But you can experience the relationship of a different quality. One has to get out of the state of hating of the opposite sides of duality. This is a process of integration of duality. You start to understand that both man and woman are just two sides of one coin, and that this coin is inside of you. If, as a man, you try to destroy a woman, or as a woman you try to destroy your man, you destroy yourself. **In reality, the internal woman represents feelings, while the internal man is logic.** That is what man and woman inside of us represent. **On the level of low vibrations, logic is harsh, stone-like, and linear. Emotions are primitive, animalistic.** The opposites of such qualities cannot integrate. What kind of understanding of each other can you have while in such widely spread polarities?

Understanding will come only on the level when intellect becomes flexible, capable of accepting any position, and when emotions move to the feelings of higher vibrations, to unconditional love. When intellect moves to the stage of awareness of itself, and feelings to the stage of unconditional love, they fuse and become one. Then there is no question of who should accept whom, as one and another are the same. But we need to get there.

Imagine a pyramid. If you happen to be in the lower vibrations, it is similar to being on the bottom—the sides of the pyramid do not touch. When you move up to the highest point of the pyramid, its four sides start to get closer and closer together, eventually coalescing at one point at the summit. In order to get to the summit, you need to get to the top of the pyramid moving all the way from the bottom. That is what the connection of the mind and the heart is. Those are the two opposite civilizations I spoke about in the beginning of our seminar. Love—Wisdom is feeling, and Godly Will of the Mind is logic.

I want to emphasize, a man is logic and intellect, while a woman is feeling. The level of their development may be very different. Only their supreme development, which is possible for a human being during the training called "Solar System," allow them to unite. Until that moment, you will only experience different degrees of a state of loneliness.

— *Today I felt totally alone. I experienced this state of complete loneliness.*

— Logic alone is deadly. Intellect without feelings is deadly. You can be very strong physically and intellectually, but what will you bring? You will bring destruction. Take a look at these supermen, so popular in the movies. They can be very strong, intelligent, but they do not have the feeling of Unconditional Love. Their feelings are at the level of animals, at the level of war for survival. If your emotional center is fully worked up, you can be a saint. You may feel Unconditional Love but be unable to say anything. You will sit in a meditating or praying position transmitting high vibrations, but when asked a question would not be able to say anything. This is a stupid saint.

116

Our way connects the mind and the heart. It occurs in a stepwise fashion. It is an ascent. This is the essence of our process, which consists of many steps. You cannot jump all the way to the top from the bottom. This is the process of constant awareness and feelings with partners that will mirror to us that side of us that is currently underdeveloped. Of course, you can sit there dreaming about a prince on a white horse who will come and take you away. But you are going to have what you have. You always meet people who reflect your own parts, but do you see it? One needs to be aware of what is going on right now. Every human being that is near you offers you an opportunity to see something in yourself. It is not going to be simple, but without it you would not be able to assemble yourself.

— *Yesterday while walking home, I laughed a lot and talked loudly. Laura said, "Can you talk less?" Suddenly, I saw two sides of me. One displays many emotions while another is thoughtful. She said that when one talks a lot, one cannot be aware. It was very interesting to observe.*

— To observe what?

— *I was in such state, laughing and describing what I saw here when we were fighting. I saw these fighters inside me. I am all bubbly and happy telling her what I saw, and she helps me to slow down.*

— Your woman is at the level of a girl who laughs first and then starts to cry. I am not saying that this is good or bad. It is what it is. Your inner man is interesting. When he says something, that is how it is going to be. And they cannot find a middle ground: a man who hammers everyone, and a girl who is overwhelmed by emotions.

— *I have a similar question. My relationship with my husband is very similar. He is very far from what I am doing here, and he constantly repeats that this is a fake. I try to talk to him, but he just sits there*

117

silently. I see that he is in pain, but I look at the situation philosophically. I understand that my inner harmony will eventually be reflected on him. I understand that my vibrations go to him. I understand that he is not comfortable. He is distraught. I do not feel guilty. I don't feel angry.

— Is that so? Perhaps you hold him responsible? Perhaps you are angry at him? Let's call things their proper names. I was in those high vibrations and after the seminars they got even higher. I came home where he was sitting not understanding anything. I showered him with those vibrations, but he was just sitting there not having a clue. He told me I was an idiot. He told me I went where I was not supposed to go to. I explained to him that I was showering him in my high vibrations that he could not withstand. The higher my vibrations went, the angrier he got. I, on the other hand, got stronger. The worse he got, the better I got. My high state showed how high my vibrations were. He did not perceive them, but I did not get angry with him, as he a "sleeper."

— *I understand that unless I understand myself inside…*

— And I would not understand until I continue to enforce the pride of my "highly spiritual" part on him.

— *I see him as a part of me.*

— We can see a very sly mechanism of duality at work here. You do not have to simply see him as a "sleeper," but you can enforce the pride of your "not-sleeping" side by blaming him for his mechanicality and sleep. Then it is not empathy but blame that maintains your illusory superiority, i.e. the internal separation.

— *I experienced certain moments of tuning in and those moments were very interesting. I noticed that by changing myself, I feel how my relationship with another person changes, i.e. how he changes. I can really see miraculous changes and experience some satisfaction in passing this very small step.*

— **Nobody gets together without a reason. People get together based on oppositions. He reflects a certain part of you that you do not accept in yourself, and he would hunt and follow you. If not him, it is going to be someone similar, until you learn to accept your own part that you project onto him. What irritates you in him is what you do not accept in yourself. What irritates you in him? What do you blame him for?**

— *He is always silent and I am constantly talking.*

What does a silent one talk about

— I speak about highly spiritual matters and he is viperously silent. Correct?

— *I don't necessarily talk about spiritual matters. Sometimes one comes home and just spills out one's emotional state.*

— **You cannot talk unless he is quiet. If he starts to talk, you would need to be quiet, and you would move into his state.**

— *Currently, we are both silent.*

— Because there is nothing to talk about. Because if one is talking, another is bound to be silent, and soon, both get old.

— *Yes.*

— What is the duality here?

— *I see this duality. One is very talkative, and another is very quiet. So, we need to move to…*

— Okay, I am talkative. Can we call what we discuss here irrelevant?

— *No.*

— No. So, there are different conversations, and to say that someone is quiet or talkative does not mean much. It is a very superficial view. One can be quiet about many different things, while another can be talkative about a number of things.

— *I used to communicate with another man, and it was different. It was neither silence nor conversation. We simply sat there quietly. We understood each other. I would say one word and he would complete it with another.*

— Where is this guy? Why did he disappear?

— *A situation came up, and he had to leave.*

— So, he did not stay with you long.

— *Yes, there was a break up. I was shown that it was enough. I had to receive a new opposite experience. But now I understand how easily two people can communicate.*

— Look, the basic point here is not talkative—silent, but what do you talk about or what are you silent about. When we start to think about what we talk about and what we are silent about, we get deeper into our problem. So, what do you talk about and what are you silent about? I can say definitely that he is silent about what you talk about.

— *When I ask certain questions, he is simply silent.*

— The level of your conversation is dividing, not connecting. It pertains to both of you.

— *And what kind of duality is here?*

— We investigate. Right now, we get to the point that one talks and another is silent. And this is normal, because if I were to talk and you were to talk at the same time, we would not get anywhere. When one is talking, other people quietly listen. But one can be silent differently. Similarly, one can talk differently. One can be silently thinking about you going to hell or one can be silently thinking about how interesting what you are saying is. One can also be silent about how boring all of this is and plan to escape.

Behind this silence and behind this talk there are certain states. And it is the interaction of these states that gives birth to the illusions of a conflict. Please, pay attention here; I did not say "conflict." I said the "illusions of a conflict." You happen to be on different poles, and you are unable to find any points of contact. This is a fact.

— *Well, there is a monologue and a dialogue. Sometimes I just want to talk to another human being soul to soul. Sometimes I can listen for hours.*

— You cannot understand what is behind the conversation. You constantly place an accent on the external expression of your states: silent—talkative.

— *This is all superficial. Physically, this is how it's expressed, but internally it is totally different.*

— **Let's touch on the most important thing here—the states. You do not even touch them. I constantly show you that behind what you call a conversation about silence and talkativeness, there are certain states. So, what are those states? What is your state? What is his state? You do not talk about it at all. Do you see that?**

— *I do not want to talk about it.*

— If you do not want to talk about it, we don't have anything to talk about.

— *No. I am not going to bring it up now.*

— Then what can we talk about? Then we are going to drop to the superficial level that I just showed you.

— *I have to sort it out myself. I am trying to sort out what in reality is going on. It is quite deep. I need to enter it.*

— If you cannot even touch it, how are you going to enter it? I am slowly bringing you toward it, and you say, "No, we

121

are not going to go further." And he does not want to touch the main thing either. So, you sit in the same state: "I am not going to discuss it." How can one understand anything here? Understanding occurs on the basis of something in common, but there is nothing in common. What do you have in common? Of course, you can get to your kitchen, grab a fork, and say, "fork." You can take a knife and say, "knife." How long can this go on?

— *Once, I thought this problem was solved. I realize now, it was just suppressed. When I come home late at night, I am afraid of him physically hurting me. I have such a difficult time explaining where I go and what I do. He cannot understand it.*

— You can say, "I go to the seminars."

— *I explain. I am honest. And I see his square eyes and a question: "Have you been fucked there?"* — *"That was not on the program,"* I reply, *"but I don't know the plans for the future."*

— He has his own understanding. He is talking about himself. This is his level of perception of life.

— *Then my life is the same.*

— I am talking about him now. For him, when people of the opposite sex get together, what else is there to do but to fuck? However, we don't know what follows in his scenario. Afterwards, we probably have to leave as the whole diapason of interactions is exhausted, except to get into a fight or to get drunk. So, he asks, "Did you drink?" — "No." "Did you fight?" — "No." What else is there? "Did you fuck?" — "No." Then, what did you do? Then it is a cult.

— *As I sit here listening to you, I enter my own situation. I come home, grab my husband, and tell him, "I am going to tell you the main theme of our seminar." I am sure he understands me. Sometimes he says, "Let me have couple shots of vodka. I will understand you better." I can't explain to him what happens here, he would not understand.*

— And you yourself, do you understand what is going on here? This is a very interesting question. How can you discuss something you yourself do not understand? In order to do so, you need to understand what you do not understand. That's what we started our conversation with.

— I am sure he understands and that he does not understand at the same time.

— You do not understand that you do not understand. And at the same time, you think that if you know, he knows also, and you start searching for the knowledge of what you do not know in yourself in him. And the darkness gets darker.

— I have finally come to understand that this is in me. There is nothing external here. It is all inside of me. I project the incomprehension I have on him. Then I say that he does not understand anything. And this is my husband. What a horror!

— I gave him my best years.

— That is why I say that our training is training in the training of your life. I repeat, this reality is a big training ground, and you cannot escape it. Our training will help you to see what that other, big training, i.e. your life is made of. But the basics have to be passed through in the big training. Here you get the jolts of awareness that help you to sort out the major problems of your life.

— Can the person next to me change when I understand something? Some kind of wave goes toward him? Or is it my own projection?

— Please, let him be. Look, your thoughts are constantly directed toward making something great out of him in order for you to look at him and feel your greatness. You can feel your own and his greatness only through yourself.

— And if I want to…

— To kill him?

— No. Well, yes.

— You already have it. Moreover, you already realize it, but being afraid of punishment, you hide it. This is your war with each other that lasts until death. A woman usually lives longer. A man will die faster and she will scream and pull out her hair, recalling good old memories and having chronic nostalgia.

— *Strawberry gum.*

— And to every next "idiot" who will show up in her life, she will announce that the one she had before was better. She will specifically explain that the previous one was a saint, that he cannot even be compared.

— *There was a show here yesterday, and everyone felt it. I was amazed when a girl said about me: "He is neither meat nor fish." And I was exactly "neither meat nor fish." I saw this aimless game that I cannot comprehend. Everyone carries his own mask.*

— In order to take off our masks, we need to see what is behind them. If you think there is nothing behind your mask, you will hold it very tight because it is the only thing with which you associate yourself. Everything else simply does not exist. So, the process of taking off masks occurs when you start to penetrate deep inside yourself and see what is behind these masks. You cannot become aware of the masks unless you find something else inside, and live through this something.

— *Yes. The mask is always on.*

— What is your mask? If I cannot say anything about my mask, I cannot even touch it. There is a huge distance between me taking off the mask and me touching the mask. If I do not touch it, I cannot say anything about it. Awareness is an opportunity to see your masks, but you do not want even to look at them. At the same time, I talk and talk and repeat the same things that come out of this fake mask. That is all one does. So, what kind of a mask is on you right now? I ask a question that questions your notion of who you are. And how do you react to this?

— *I am not sure.*

— You do not react at all.

— *Insincerely.*

— This is your explanation but not the answer to my question. I asked what kind of mask you display now.

— *I don't know.*

— Look how the mind is made up. He is not aware of what he himself is saying.

— *I am neither...*

— It is a mask. I am afraid to touch it. What does this mean, "I am neither"? I am such. And how such are you? Well, such. No, you are neither. No, you know I am such and such. I am great, and you are nothing...

In order to have pride, one does not even need to think. I am bigger than you and that is all I need to be full of pride. I am bigger than you, woman. And what is a woman? I don't even know, but I know for sure, I am bigger. You are a prostitute, and I am a properly brought up independent woman. I don't even know what woman is, but I am a strong woman. That is our market talk.

— *I am a woman of the east.*

— East, west, south-west ... If west is taken, I move to south-west. I am a great woman of the south-west. I am a northern playboy's dream. I don't know him, but I will wait for him. He is going to come, and we are going to be happy.

I invite you to ascend to somewhat higher level of vibrations and to take a look at what happens to you in the lowest vibrations. What do you see?

— *I saw that the negative I see in people that are close to me is mine.*

125

— I was excited by my relationship with a very close woman, and I saw why it disintegrated. I refused to play a certain role, a role of the father. I did it quite consciously. I refused to play the role of her father.

— A woman frequently does not know what it means to be a woman. She may look not for a husband, but for a father. She may want to be a daughter. She may try to recreate this scenario with her husband: I am a daughter, and my husband is my father. But then she will move to a mother role, and he will become her son. That is how the paternal scenario is recreated. Blame and guilt are usually behind this. **But you cannot come into a contact with another human being without entering the image he is currently in. Otherwise, you will not be able to interact with him at all.**

Look what happens here. In order to establish some kind of relationship with another human being, one needs to understand the image he or she is currently in.

— We have touched upon a topic of a man and a woman present inside every single human being. I wanted to see why my husband is silent. My inquiry was to see my inner man and my inner woman. He is silent because he is being hit for every word he says.

— He knows that if he is to say something, he is going to be struck down.

— I liked men that talk little. I thought they complete me. I talk a lot. I am more active, and they are quiet, silent. Now I understand why they are so quiet.

— In reality, there is an inner child inside each man and each woman, a child that is resentful. Take a look at how boys and girls interact. A boy likes a girl. He may throw a book at her or pull her hair. Then grown up boys and girls get together in a teacher's room and reprimand them. Later on, they call in boys and girls that are called parents and reprimand them also. So, everybody reprimands everybody. And the reason for the

126

reprimand will always be found. I scold you because I love you, and I resent you because I love you. This is what we call love here.

CHAPTER 3

TO INVESTIGATE MYSELF MEANS TO SEE MY EXPERIENCE

•◆•

In blaming yourself, you do not accept your experience

— Who is going to start today's meeting?

— *Yesterday you said that before we can talk about higher levels of consciousness we need to think what kind of shit we are sitting in. That is how I understood you.*

— I want you to understand my terminology correctly. Calling something shit presupposes a need to clean oneself from it. Every word carries a certain meaning and a certain emotional weight. The word "shit" happens to be accusatory and unaccepting. By talking about something and calling it shit, you condemn it. **When you condemn something, you feel guilty about it.** That's how you get into the malignant circle of condemnation and guilt. In reality, this is your experience. If you condemn it, you do not accept yourself. So, there is your experience and your relation to it. Moreover, this experience is you. Describing your experience with words that carry blame and condemnation leads to your own separation.

When you call something shit, you condemn it. And you may not even understand what you are condemning. "I am so good and he is shit,"—you can think. We would not get far this way. I brought up this example as it pertains to everyone. We cannot investigate the experience we received if we consider it to be shit. If we consider something to be shit, we would not even discuss it. You will be interested to find out who is clean here and how this clean one will look at your shit. There is no shit here, just experience. Any experience you have lived through, are living through, and will live through irrespective of whether it was betrayal, jealousy, hysterics, craziness, anything you want, is present in each one of us to a degree. And if it is not yet present, it will be.

If you would relate to something as if to a piece of dirt, you need to be ashamed and hide from everyone, you would not be able to see yourself holistically. Here we work with what you call shit, dirt, and darkness. This is not bad. This is our experience, and there would not be any spiritual development without it. That is why we came here.

— *There is a prayer: let the door be locked behind the evil. I can see now that it is quite one-sided. There is evil out there, and we locked the door on it.*

— Everything is right when you see it right. Yes, certain low vibrations that we call evil or the creation of the essences of the Dark Circle do exist. From their point of view, those vibrations are good. But our work leads to an increase in the vibrations of human consciousness. As you accumulate the higher vibrations, you graduate from the old matrix of consciousness as a baby graduates from diapers. Diapers are good for a small child, but an adult does not need them. He has grown out of them. Those who do not work to increase the vibrations of their consciousness remain in the old matrix and continue to accumulate the old experiences.

We happen to be on the frontier. There is so-called light and so-called darkness here, or so-called evil and so-called goodness. But those are technical terms that describe the duality of a given reality. Meanwhile, many people who happen to be here, in this reality, replace the technical description of the so-called negative side of duality by its condemnation. When we judge something as disgusting, as something that cannot be accepted and discussed, we cannot advance in investigating the dual nature of this reality.

We need to see it. But you will only be able to see it when you de-identify with your own false personality that is built dually. In order to do so, you need to track down both sides of your personality, <u>verbalizing</u> the results of your self-investigation. When you see and speak out loud both sides of your personality, you have an opportunity to exit the dual perception. That is what this prayer implies. When you move from the first floor to the second floor using an elevator, the first floor remains behind when you arrive at the second floor. When you get to the third floor, both the first and the second floors are behind you. And that is how it goes.

Self-investigation of the roles

— I asked myself a question: "What kind of a woman am I?" I already discussed my woman, and I told you what she does with her internal man. The more I try to be woman-mother, woman-wife, woman-daughter, and the more I try to be good everywhere, the more I am unable

to get anything done as a result. The more I try to be good, the less successful I become at experiencing a feeling of nothingness as a result. I start to feel resentment toward those for whom I do it.

— Pay attention, you said, "I am nothing." Nothing is nothing, i.e. it does not exist. But you exist. And what are you now? If you can see what you are now, it is the answer to your question. If you are unable to see it, you will consider yourself nothing. Every one of us has a mask with which he has identified. It is only possible to remove this mask by using self-investigation.

You have to talk about yourself with an understanding that you talk about your *persona*. The one who starts to honestly discuss where he is and what he considers himself to be frees himself from this mask. The only way to exit the false notion about yourself is to talk about yourself while understanding that you don't describe yourself. You describe your mask, your image. When you talk about your masks, you start to understand that you are a being that is changing. This is very important to understand.

— *I allowed myself to be bad, and it appears to me that I am getting out.*

— I allowed myself to see duality, a contradiction of my personality. But you cannot see it until you understand that what you call "bad" is just a certain role that is opposite to the so-called "good" role. Good cannot exist without bad, and bad cannot exist without good. Kind cannot exist without spiteful, and spiteful without kind. In this dual world, the oppositions always walk hand in hand.

— *Yes, but I did not want to see my "bad" side before. I was trying to convince myself that I would do better, I would strive harder. But the result was the same.*

— Conduct an investigation of yourself being bad. What does bad mean? How bad are you? In what exact way are you bad? You will find out that what is bad for one is good for somebody else. You will see that "bad" and "good" are relative notions. But first, you need to figure out what it was that you did not want to see. What did you consider to be bad? What did you not want to see in yourself?

— *I tried not to see how I abandoned my family to go to the seminar. I consider myself to be the egoist leaving my family and coming here. They would be sitting there starving in the cold...*

— I would rather torture them at home. Will that be the highest declaration of my love to them, or will that show my egoism?

— *It will show my egoism.*

— But I consider going to the seminar to be an act of egoism, and staying home torturing them not to be egoistic.

— *One more thing about my mask. My mask is bordering on clown behavior.*

— Okay. Look, I am inserting my comments into your story in order to clarify certain details. It's good that you have talked certain things through already, but you need to see more and more details. If you use the words "good," "bad," "I did not want to see myself as bad, and now I am ready to see myself as bad," my question will be: "What is "bad" for you?" Tell me exactly how bad and in what particular bad way did you not want to see yourself previously, and are ready to see yourself now.

The minuteness of investigation characterizes our process of self-investigation. This is the ability to discern. Words are so used up here that it is almost impossible to understand what they mean. Nobody clarifies them because that leads to even greater misunderstanding. The ability to discern presupposes a highly developed intellect.

— *To see the whole out of one part?*

— To see a part from the whole. For example, you say, "Here is an automobile." "What is an automobile?" I ask you. "Well, it is a red automobile." "What is an automobile?" I ask you again. But you cannot say anything.

— *We deconstruct it to pieces.*

— We start to investigate it. Take a textbook that describes how an automobile is made. You would learn that it has a transmission, a fuel system, an electric system, etc. Each system consists of a certain number of parts.

— *When I see a carburetor, I can say that it is from Ford. Is that right?*

— Prior to saying where it came from, we need to sort out for what purpose a carburetor is made. What function in an automobile does it carry?

— *That will allow us to see the whole picture.*

— Yes, that's the vision on the level of a mechanic, who is not simply driving a car but fixes and maintains it. He will not say, "Well, we have an automobile here, and something is broken in it." He has to figure out what is broken, why is it broken, and how to fix it. In order to do that, he needs to know how an automobile is assembled and different methods to repair it. A human being is a much more complicated structure than an automobile. A human being does not know himself. Awareness is an opportunity to investigate ourselves in order to learn who we are.

— *We have only two or three thoughts about ourselves.*

— What do you mean "we"?

— *Me.*

— Then say so, because I have more thoughts.

— *You mean, in order to become aware of oneself, one needs to see more out of less?*

— What does it mean, "more out of less"? You are talking rubbish. This is a typical situation. More, less, better, longer, green, yellow… You need to see you speak rubbish. I spoke to you about it yesterday and I repeat again, you speak rubbish.

— *I understand that in order to hear the correct answer, one needs to formulate the correct question.*

— At this point you are unable to formulate the correct question. I say that you speak rubbish because you look outside instead of looking inside. All your words are connected to you looking for something outside. When I say this is rubbish, you would not be able to do anything this way, you would not find what you are looking for. But you continue. I repeat. This is rubbish. If you want to find yourself, look inside. But in order to do so, you need to start to figure out how you are assembled.

I introduce you to certain aspects of this work. What we learn is different from learning how the physical body is assembled using an anatomy atlas. The physical body is something that does not really exist. In cosmic terminology, the physical body is called "that, that does not exist," because it is an illusion. But here, the physical body is the only thing that is real, the only thing that exists. That is a paradox. People think that it is the only thing that exists, but for Cosmic Consciousness, it is something that does not exist.

It is not enough to hear something new.
One needs to experience it

— I was contemplating on the question of human suffering, and I had a revelation: suffering is inside me.

— Everything is inside.

— But one needs to see that this suffering is also inside. I understood that suffering occurs as a consequence of two opposite sides of duality fighting each other. I was shaken by the fact that I did not see it before. It is so obvious. By seeing it, I understood that I had a question for this answer.

— Exactly. I constantly talk about it, and you have heard it many times before. But you experienced it just now. **This is awareness: when new knowledge connects and gets experienced.** As a result of this internal experience, she understood what I meant when I was talking about it. This is very important. You listen to what I say many times. You have the impression that I repeat myself all the time. It appears to you that you know it, but I keep repeating it. But when asked, you cannot say anything about it. Meanwhile, you have a strong notion that you know it. "I heard these words many times," you say.

Your conditioned mind is tuned in to register the repetitiveness of what has happened before. It does not look for anything new but looks for what happened before. "He wore those socks before. What a bore. He used these words before. He repeats himself." That is the level of your perception. **The inner state you are in determines what you see outside**. If a deadly boredom is inside of you, you will see it outside. Certain things will happen around you all the time, but you will be bored and not interested.

Our work is two-sided. I cannot make someone aware just because he listens to me. It is impossible. Nobody is able to do it. I create opportunities. Will you use them? This is the question. In order to answer this question, one needs to become aware of how one's perception is made and learn how to change it. The only thing you can become aware of now is that your boredom is connected to the tuning of your perception. It is not easy to become aware of it, as it is global for you. You have identified with it completely. For you, this is not a small episode.

It happens that one is bored during the day, but then he gets into another state. For him, this is just an episode. For you, it is constant. Your identification with it is very strong, and what one is strongly identified with is extremely difficult to see.

So, how can you see it? A human being who is identified with a certain state does not see it. One is simply in it, mechanically. So, start to use the opportunity presented here. Start talking through your states. You started to say that everything is the same and boring. Excellent. I caught your state and returned it to you. I say, "Look, this is a result of the tuning of your perception. You can see it from another side now."

You can become aware of this now, or you can miss it. But an opportunity appeared. You can be silent about it. Many people are. What is going on inside of them? Who knows? They don't know themselves. A certain sensation appears inside them. One is interesting and another is boring, or certain wandering thoughts appear, but they are not aware of them, as **to become aware means to see them from a side**. In order to become aware you need to exit the habitual state and to see it from a side. But you are submerged in it, and that is why you don't even see it.

We create opportunities here. And if you want to use these opportunities, you have to start talking through your states. When you start to talk through your states, you can at least hear what you talk about. This is not easy, but I will catch what you say and return it to you saying, "Look, that's where you are now." That is how an opportunity to become aware of what you are in is created. My task is to create an opportunity for you to talk through your states and to return it back to you in order for you to see the states you are in. To see means to look from a side. You cannot see your own state while you are submerged in it. Is that understood?

— *I want to talk through my state. Yesterday we discussed a relationship between a husband and a wife. I listen quietly, and I was thinking how it mirrors the situation with my wife. It was very interesting to see myself from another side.*

— And what precisely was it mirroring?

— *I am engrossed with spiritual development, while my wife is completely uninterested. I bring her books, but she does not read them. She constantly complains about something. One of the participants asked me how I was doing today. I answered, "I am fine." Suddenly, he got very angry and said, "Fine. Fine. Is everything really fine with you?" I reflected for a while and then said, "Well, of course not everything is fine with me, but if I were to start telling you about this..." I saw that I did not want to discuss it. So, what happens then? Certain work needs to be done. Where will we get if we continue to pretend that everything is fine?*

— What are the steps of spiritual development? There are people who are not interested in spiritual development at all. They have their own notions of life: to make more money, to climb up a social ladder, to eat at a better restaurant. That's how they live. There are people who need something else. They start reading esoteric literature and go to spiritual retreats. They develop a feeling: "I am not the way everyone around me is. I am different." This is not clear. Who am I? They start thinking, "Am I Buddha's reincarnation? Am I Christ? Which planet am I from?" I am not saying that this is bad. I just describe how it happens. At that time, their habitual life can start deteriorating. But they get pulled toward this other world, stronger and stronger. That may ruin their family and financial situation. At the same time, their certainty in their difference gets stronger.

Everybody else is material and I am spiritual. That type of pride is very common. Religion considers it to be a sin. **To me, the only sin is not to be aware.** What is called sin here is the opposite side of duality. It is opposite to what is called virtue. Awareness allows you to investigate the mechanisms of interactions of the opposite sides of duality.

For example, what is pride? It has many faces. Many talk about the necessity of fighting one's pride. These are just common phrases, as any fight just reinforces what one is fighting with. **How does pride appear?** What is the mechanism of its appearance? Unless you understand how it appears and how it works, you will not be able to do anything about it. So, how does it appear? Why does it have so many faces? Why is it so persistent?

— *I am different from everyone else.*

— Everyone is different and not the same as everyone else.

— *I am better.*

— *Pride appears because one identifies with a certain duality. When one shows one side of this duality, the side one likes, one considers himself higher than the rest.*

— Yes. Pride is a consequence of activation of certain dualities, and because everything here is dual, it is impossible to avoid pride. Pride may appear as a result of activation of the duality "beautiful—ugly." This is an important duality for many personalities. I look at another woman thinking that she is ugly while I am beautiful. That is a specific pride which is based on the duality connected to beauty. We can look at the duality "smart—stupid." They are stupid, I am smart. But oops, someone appears who is smarter than me, and jealousy based on the pride of the mind is turned on in me. Another common duality for any spiritual seeker is "spiritual—material." Other people appear to be totally material to you. Suddenly, someone more spiritual shows up and what happens? Jealousy. And what can you do with it?

Commonly offered recommendations are to fight the pride, to accept it, or to repent are built on a one-sided vision of duality. As the mechanism of duality is hidden, all these recommendations don't help. You think you have caught your pride, but it just moved and transformed into something else. So, first you have to see how it appears and how what you are about to fight is maintained. In order to do so, you need to understand the dual nature of your personality and its dual perception of the surrounding world. When you start to apply this knowledge to yourself, you will see the mechanisms of your ego at work. When you see these mechanisms, you can exit them. If you don't see them, you are these mechanisms. These mechanisms are very sly.

How does pride appear?

— Pride appears as a result of one's identification with one part of a duality, and associated contempt and antagonism toward another side. Take a look at your own pride. The pride of the so-called spiritual people is connected to spirituality. A spiritual person activates the duality "spiritual—material" and experiences pride by comparing himself with non-spiritual people, who are not right, who don't know, don't understand, and who are not aware. In identifying oneself with one side of a particular duality, one fights its opposite side. **That's how experience is accumulated in every duality.**

You identify with one side and start fighting the opposite side, mechanically acquiring the experience connected with a particular duality. Take a look at religious wars and crusades that are led to fight the infidel. The same thing can be seen in every war, which reflects the feud between the opposite sides of ethnic, religious, political, economic, cultural, and other dualities.

— *"True—False."*

— Wait. We need to get to the "True" first. We have to figure out how the mechanism of duality functions. Until we understand it, we will not understand anything, because "True—false" is another duality. Everything here is a result of mentation of the conditioned mind. Perception that people consider to be real comes precisely from the dual nature of the conditioned mind. Until we understand the working mechanisms of duality, we will not understand ourselves.

— *I mentioned the wars against infidels. That is what I meant in asking about "True—false."*

— Yes, "True—False," "Faithfull—Unfaithful," "Right—Wrong." Crusaders used to say, "Accept Jesus or die!" It is under this slogan that the the conversion of infidels to Christians occurred.

— *Crusaders were killing Muslims and Jews.*

141

— Look, everything that happens here is based on the dual perception that gives birth to feud and war. We are currently investigating how pride appears through the prism of duality "Spiritual—Material." I come home, and I find my wife there who does not want to understand the subject that I consider to be highly spiritual. I bring her books, but she does not want to read them.

I come home and find my husband there. I start talking about the seminar I attended, but he does not want to listen. Is that correct? Everyone here talks about it. It happens to every one of you.

Why does it happen? It happens because a certain duality gets activated. In order for you to receive the experience of one side of the duality, you need to have the opposite side. That's why this situation appears. That is exactly how it should be. You should have two poles: one of them you identify with, another you project onto someone else, usually onto people who are close to you. Unless you have the material pole in front of your eyes, you will not understand that you are spiritual.

— I have just felt that it was me who created the situation where my father is very material. My mother does not understand what is going on here very well, even though she tries hard. My sister tries too. I thought I wanted them to understand and to become spiritual, but I can see now that, in reality, I don't want this to happen, because it is with them on the background that I can feel myself as spiritual. If they become spiritual, I will not feel that way.

— Now you can see that your spirituality is, in reality, a pseudo-spirituality. As you can see, self-investigation can lead to shocking discoveries.

— This is not spirituality. This is pride that is based on the ground of intelligence.

142

— Let's not mix "Smart—Stupid" and "Spiritual—Material." These are two different dualities. Look, I am pointing out a contradistinction to you. This is a very subtle contradistinction that is not easy to catch. You say, "I am so smart!" "And what is smart?" I ask. "Well, spiritual." – "And what is spiritual?" Everything is mixed in one pile. Let's separate. The duality "smart—stupid" is activated everywhere and all the time irrespective of whether one considers himself to be spiritual or not.

— *The mind tries to show itself of in every sphere.*

— Is what I discuss smart or stupid? Is it spiritual or material?

— *It is what it is. It is a fact.*

— *We do not know what certain notions mean. So, we constantly get up and fight, not even understanding what we are fighting for.*

— A human being has three types of reactions: physical, emotional, and mental. We need to become aware of each one of them. Our goal is to harmonize the human apparatus so it can function properly. This occurs by balancing the dualities that were activated in order to acquire the necessary experience. Is that clear?

— *Yes.*

Understanding duality is inseparable from understanding yourself

— One's intellect, feelings, and bodily sensations have to be highly developed to do this work. In order to understand the work of dualities, you have to be good at discernment. You can start to discern only after you have acquired a vast experience in the sphere you investigate. It's important to be able to discern different dualities and to discern their opposite sides.

What is the difference between spiritual and material, smart and stupid? Try to answer this question on the emotional level. This is going to be very difficult, as these notions are usually appraised on the intellectual level. But there is also an emotional aspect to them. That is why understanding the work of dualities requires the development of the emotional, intellectual, and moving centers. In the state you are currently in, you are not capable of understanding this. In order to understand our work, we need to develop intellectual, emotional, and moving centers. As they develop, we will understand more and more about ourselves.

You cannot say you understand everything now. You can say that you understand only at the level of perception that is based on the current state of development of your psychic centers. When you start to develop them, their understanding will grow. Their understanding is not fixed. I understood that two multiplied by two is four and that is it. Wake me up in the morning, and I will say that two multiplied by two is four. That is not going to happen here. Today, two by two is four, and tomorrow, on the higher level of consciousness, you may suddenly see that two by two is five.

The false personality lives on account of activation of dualities that constitute its structure. Activation of these dualities occurs mechanically. We can say it just happens. The false personality itself does not understand how it activates it, it just does it. You need to become aware of how exactly this activation occurs. What does it mean to become aware of something? It means to start seeing the working mechanisms of false personality in yourself. It is activation of the dualities that brings you suffering, problems, and what pushes you to search for yourself.

We can see that activation of the dualities proceeds through certain consistent patterns. When you activate a certain duality, for example, "spiritual—material," you start to accumulate experience in connection with it. At the time, you do not understand exactly what spiritual is. You start to touch upon this subject. There are many books on the subject that you can spend your entire life reading. There is a constant influx of new spiritual currents, avatars, saints, and gurus. You do not know where to look.

So, this is what happens with the activation of the duality "spiritual—material." At the same time, you start to feel strong pressure from the opposite side of this polarity, from the material, as in order to understand that you are spiritual you need to push off the material. The material side starts to irritate you. "I am a spiritual being. What do I need money for? Why do I need to do this boring work for the benefit of society? Why do I have all those material people around me? I cannot even talk to anyone. I come home and what do I see? My wife and my kids are also material." That is the opposite side and it is staring you right in your face. So I, a highly developed spiritual being, have to live with those spiritually underdeveloped creatures. Our old relationships—familial and social—start to shake.

— *I started to look for people who are similar.*

— You start reading spiritual literature, attend lectures and retreats. You need to investigate the spiritual side. At the same time, activation of the duality occurs, and material becomes even more material. Your wife and your kids start to become more and more distant as they are only occupied by the material side. The more spiritual you become, the more distant they become. This is a process of stretching of duality. **This is a law.** That is how it should be. But it causes irritation in you as you have pride. You are spiritual. And the more spiritual you are, the higher your pride. This pride leads to irritation and escalation of conflict.

That is how your "spiritual" part fights with the "material" part. At the same time, it appears to you that you try to teach them spirituality. You have read the book and start to tell your husband that the world is multidimensional. He does not give a damn about it. "Where have you been? Who have you been with? Have you screwed anyone there?" That is what interests him. You start to explain to him that you did not screw anyone and that the world is multidimensional. But he is not interested in the multidimensionality of the world. He is interested in whether you fucked someone or not. So, you break some dishes and get into complete materiality. You start blaming yourself for this total downfall into the material sphere. But it is difficult to blame yourself for a long time, and you start to blame the one who, you think, is the cause of this downfall.

This leads to the escalation of a conflict inside your family that is not very stable as it is. Kids look at it and start crying, as their interests are connected to the actualization of completely different dualities, which you are not capable of satisfying due to your interest in your own activated dualities. All this is quite lawful and needs to be experienced. You cannot skip this experience, as otherwise you will not be able to experience the duality "spiritual—material." On top of it, the process of acquisition of this experience is not fast. You read spiritual literature and you want to discuss it. Certain people appear with whom you can at least discuss it. A certain circle of people appears, or you might get in some circles where you think you are being understood.

Usually, those are certain groups, cults, confessions that unite people of certain types. For example, some get together under a slogan: "Jesus is alive and with us." A few more slogans that everyone agrees with, and everyone is happily dancing, kissing, and hugging. You join in.

Some are interested in something more intellectual: hollotrop breathing, gestalt therapy, psychodrama, NLP, etc. Today's psychology provides a wide assortment of options. One can get sucked into there. You start to perfect yourself. You start to lead a group. You start to make money doing it. You are in it. But if you have a passion for self-investigation, you would not be satisfied with this. You will see that all of those things represent fragments. You will see that you have received a necessary experience, and now it's time to move on. You can move through those fragments at a very high speed. You start trying something else. You go through this and that, and you feel that neither this nor that is of interest to you. You enter something else, and again you find that this is not it. So, you enrich yourself by experiencing these fragments until you find a place which offers a real opportunity to see these fragmented pieces of your experience as a whole.

— *At the end, this will turn into "not it" again.*

— I call the process that occurs here "holistic psychology." Holistic means whole. Holistic psychology investigates and views a human being as part of the Whole that created it. I apply different points of view in order to investigate a human being. I stimulate you to do the same and to understand something new here. There is constant movement here.

Look at the esoteric, psychological, religious, and philosophical movements. Many of them are very strict. These movements represent certain conceptions that are being somewhat modified but, in essence, remain unchanged. Either by yourself or through a friend introducing you, you get into a certain circle. The members of this circle start to show you what this circle is about. This process is done by people who know. They are the ones who maintain this intellectual prison. They can walk you for a very long time. It may appear to you that you are near the door to enlightenment or that you have been enlightened already. In reality, this is a demarcated circle that you cannot exit, because you do not see the demarcation mark.

Here, on the other hand, I show you how these closed circles are created in a human psyche. Our main task is to become aware of these circles in ourselves and to get out of them. Our process helps you to exit out of all conditionings created in the mind. Our main goal is awareness. I am not here to download some other smart notion into your system. If I wanted to do that, I would describe a certain circle, introduce you to it, and then so-called "spiritual development" would occur within the limits of that circle. You will find none of that here. What you will find here is awareness. It will lead you to exit all your limitations. You need to become aware of what is going on inside of you.

— *My question is about external and internal. Any cult represents an external circle to which people constantly return. We, on the other hand, need to sort things out inside of us. Is that the difference?*

— As a rule, these communities do not help you to sort things out inside. They offer you a certain recipe of faith. That is why the majority of people are going there. What did you ask yesterday? "Good people, help me, what do I do now?" So, they immediately tell you what to do. Hubbard, for example. Are you familiar with scientology? They have the answers to all the questions. Learn it, and you will get the answers to all the questions. I tell you, all the questions and all the answers are in you. Then I show you that only by formulating new questions, will you arrive at new answers. I stimulate new questions in you. You need to feel a taste of self-investigation. When you experience it, you will understand why you are here. If you do not, you will not understand, and you will leave. You will go on searching further. Most likely, you will search for some readymade answers to not-formulated-by-you questions.

You scream, "Help me to be spiritual! Help me to get rid of my suffering!" You will find many people who will tell you, "What are you screaming about? Come with us. Everything is nice here. We will tell you everything." You can get stuck there. This is neither good nor bad. This shows that you need the experience they offer and points to the level of your awareness. Perhaps you need to pass it again and again. But perhaps you are ready to see things the way they are. I do not negate anything. I will never tell you, "You came here. You cannot go anywhere else."

Go wherever you need to go. But be aware. Go and take a look. What is going on there? What took you there? Become aware of it. This is a way to accelerate the accumulation of the experience you need. Our process represents an accelerated way of acquiring personal experience. Our aim is total integration of your personal experience. Awareness of oneself is the fastest way to spiritual development. I call it the extreme way of spiritual development.

Every one of us has certain areas that need to be filled with experience. This reality is a big training ground. You cannot do anything wrong here. Everything you need is here.

The question is what do you need? I ask you to feel it. Who wants to say something?

What are you looking for in sexual experience?

— *My first sexual experience lasted over three hours and was very painful. The memory of it is still with me. When I think about it, I recall the state of fear, and I feel unwell.*

— So, your sexual experience started with pain.

— *Pain. Discomfort. Restriction. That's what I remember.*

— Do you feel this now?

— *Yes.*

— Is sex pleasant or unpleasant for you?

— *It is both pleasant and unpleasant, but the memory that remains is unpleasant. Since then, my sexual experience was always complicated by this underlying unpleasant state. The feeling of unpleasantness remains.*

— If this is unpleasant, why do it? Nobody asks you to do it. One can live without sex. So, there should be an element of pleasure in it for you.

— *Yes.*

— What is this pleasurable element connected to?

— *It is inside. Going through sexual experience some part of me constantly searches for the unpleasant and eventually comes to pleasant state.*

— Look, this is a paradox. There is a minus and there is a plus. So, unpleasant can be pleasant. Recently, I saw a Japanese movie. A man meets a woman. They become lovers. The way they love each other is quite peculiar. They hit each other with sticks. That is how they get sexually excited.

150

— I saw this state from the side yesterday. I used to receive it. I saw it yesterday. It was horrible. I choose not to experience it again.

— If you look at their life, you can say it is horror. But this horror is happening to you. That means you need it for some reason. We came to this reality in order to acquire experience. You don't encounter anything that you don't need here. Whatever happens in your life is exactly what you need. Yes, it is easy to say that everything around you is horror and to try to forget it. But that is not the approach of the one who is aware. The aware human being understands, or at least starts to understand, that everything she creates in her life is the experience she needs in order to see and to understand herself. It is possible to integrate the experience you have and to transfer it to a different quality only by seeing precisely what the particular experience gave you, a holistic human being. What did you experience in connection with it? What did you need to learn?

— I saw that I received the experience I continued to accumulate later on in life, not knowing there was any other experience.

— Why did you choose this particular experience? What exactly did you want to take from this experience? You were looking for pain in sex. Is that right?

— I don't know.

— You said that your first sexual experience was very painful. You could have found someone with whom this experience would not have been so painful, but you chose precisely this experience.

— But later on, I continued to experience the same state I experienced the first time.

— But you have attracted it yourself. No one forced you to?

— That's correct.

— Therefore, this experience was necessary. So, what kind of experience was it? What did you feel? Did you feel yourself a victim? What was felt and sensed during that experience?

— *I felt like a victim. A similar state was experienced with my dad—the state of oppression. For me, it was normal to be oppressed in such a way.*

— So, you experienced the state of oppression. You chose this experience. Now we have to review your relationship with your father. Basic personality programs are downloaded by mother and father. Then these programs are lived through by the personality of their child. We are dealing with your experience of being oppressed, of being a victim. You were talking about a particular sphere. You were talking about your experience of these programs in the sexual sphere. But you also have this program in two other spheres: the emotional and intellectual spheres.

— *Yes.*

— You hold this theme everywhere. You came to Earth to find out what it means to be oppressed, and you have acquired a certain quantity of this experience. Do you need to continue to accumulate this experience, or do you feel ready to complete and transform it?

— *I saw that different types of experience could be chosen in the sexual sphere. I did not see it as an option in the emotional and intellectual spheres. I saw it only after you explained it. It is impossible to continue this in the sexual sphere for me, while in the emotional and intellectual spheres it is still tolerable.*

— Okay. So, what kind of experience do you choose now? You can move into the role of an oppressor and start to oppress others. However, the state of victimhood also provides an opportunity to experience empathy. From a role of an oppressor, it is very difficult to feel empathy, but from the role of a victim empathy can be felt. Victims feel and know very well what it is to experience oppression, pain, and suffering. Victims can start to feel that the oppressor also suffers, and suffers a lot.

The oppressor experiences suffering that is equal to the victim's suffering. But the oppressor refuses to acknowledge that. The oppressor refuses to be aware of his guilt, refuses to experience victimhood. This state of victimhood is destructive, and should be dropped onto the victim. Any action is directed either inside or outside. The oppressor acts out. He externalizes. He oppresses. The states of pity and guilt are opposite. These are the states of self-oppression. Anyone who oppresses another, in reality oppresses himself. But the illusion is created that one can oppress another human being without oppressing oneself. The oppressor oppresses oneself without seeing it.

The victim, on the other hand, feels the state of suffering that can transfer to a state of compassion. So, you can switch to a state of an oppressor and start doing what was done to you. In reality, you will be doing it to yourself. On the other hand, you can switch to a state of empathy. In order to do so, you need to feel empathy to those that oppressed you. You need to see all these oppressors and all the forms of oppression and rape that you lived through—sexual, emotional, mental (particularly with your father)—and to feel those people as those who experienced colossal suffering. That's what it was in reality. A human being would not oppress another human being unless he is in a state of severe suffering, a state of which he himself is not aware.

We choose a model of a winner

— Can I continue with the "father" theme? After yesterday's seminar, I feel I am in a closed up state. I want to understand where this state is coming from. I am returning to my childhood, to those years of which I try to become aware. I don't see everything. Something happened there that led me to feel hurt and to resent the whole world. I live with this pain, and as a result I close even more, building a shell.

I refuse to feel. These feelings accumulate, and then suddenly spill out into devil knows what. Sometimes this leads to the destruction of others. I almost caught one mechanism yesterday, but it escaped. I can't see where it is coming from. I can't see the reasons for it. My parents have passed away. There are no relatives who I can talk to. I would love to ask my parents, to look into their eyes, but it is impossible. I search my memory, but to no avail. Yesterday, I was able to sense my husband, a man. The theme of a man and a woman opened up, and I felt that my resentment was directed toward my father. He rejected me all my life. He drank all his life. He was always distant. He was never a man to me. He was never a human being to me. He was nobody. Suddenly, I experienced these bright flashes of memories. I felt what a girl feels in the presence of a man, some kind of protection, some kind of an ideal. But aside from profanities, I heard nothing from him. He tried to poison us with gas. Somehow I was brought back to life. And suddenly pain surfaced. I lived my whole life pretending he never existed, and suddenly I understood that he was the first man in my life. Yes, I was born of him, but he was always a man for me. I have never seen a man in him. So, I was a rejected woman from day one. I am in this state of protest from the crib, trying to prove that I am strong and smart.

— To prove that you are a man.

— Yes. And, of course, I turned out to be a man.

— I reject my inner woman. Therefore, the positive model is a man's model, and a man has to be strong. So,

154

I start to form a strong man inside me and to reject a woman in me. Later on, my husband shows it to me. He does the same thing, he rejects me. Look, whatever was downloaded by our parents, we reproduce later on in our life. So, without fully sorting out the parents, we cannot understand anything. To sort out means to come to understand that with all the negativity and awfulness of the experience we lived through with them, it was our own choice. I entered this family at this specific time, in this specific country in order to acquire the experience I need. When this is understood, I start to accept the responsibility for everything that happened to me. That is the basic moment. Otherwise, I will always look for a scapegoat. When I start to take full responsibility for everything I created and continue to create in my life from the moment I was born, I will understand what kind of experience I came here to acquire.

Special stages and scenarios were created in order for you to receive what you need. Until you understand that you have created all of this yourself, you will not be able to accept it. But then, you will not be able to sort out what is going on in your life.

— *I start to experience this pain. This experience resurfaces, and I submerge into sensations of childhood, understanding that I need to sit and to feel my inner girl that has been cast off. I understand that the further and deeper I experience these feelings, the further I close up. I understand that I descend. The door closes again, and I need to step away from it.*

— You can only conduct self-investigation in case you de-identify with all your roles: a girl, a woman, a wife, etc. If this girl is in you, the pain is in you. There is nothing else. Identification with a role leads to tears. "They have insulted

155

me. They have hurt me. Why did I come to this world?" This will continue until you continue to identify with a role. When you investigate a role, your de-identification with it increases. The more you investigate, the more you de-identify with what you investigate.

In reality, this is just a role that you chose in order to acquire a certain experience. You are simply receiving the experience of a certain role. This is it. The true "I" never judges anything out of the personality through which the acquisition of the experience occurs. But, being that personality, i.e. identifying yourself with it, you will judge and criticize everything that you think leads to your suffering. But self-investigation is not conducted based on the vision of the personality. The more you conduct self-investigation, the more you will de-identify with what you are not, i.e. with the personality and its roles.

Yes, there will be tears. Yes, painful moments will be recalled. That will help you to de-identification with the illusions of your perception of yourself. Those will not be tears of self-pity or condemnation but tears of cleansing, tears of de-identification with the experience that was acquired by you. You will cry and de-identify with the illusory image of yourself, the image that you have created here. This image took the shape, body, and perception of its own, but this image is not you.

— *But that projects onto everything I do in life. I close myself from everything around me. I close myself from work, family, and friends. I close myself from life. When a certain part leaves, I feel that something was erased. I feel lighter. Something new appears inside that wants to get a new experience. Enough is enough. How much longer can I stay in this damp, dark place? Let's move on. Something new just arrived. It is small, but it already needs new experience. This drop bumps into the same*

156

old situations and sees that it is repeating the same old thing again. I should open up, but no, I close up again. The old pain is in the way. It is a simple situation, but one has to take the first step.

— Without a new image of yourself you cannot investigate the old image.

— *I don't understand. This is not clear to me.*

— **You need a new image of yourself. It does not need to be very explicit and detailed, but it needs to be present. Take an image of yourself as a creature that does not have any relationship to this reality, but that decided to investigate it, and in order to do so, created a special spacesuit—a physical body. You were born from certain parents. You received a definitive program from them. You did it in order to live through a certain experience. You can investigate this program, understanding that you are not this program.**

When you are only a personality, you are constantly thrown between blame, guilt, and self-pity. You dangle, and nothing quantitatively new happens to you. But you came here to self-investigate. This is why you need to **create a notion of yourself** that is not related to the old matrix of consciousness. This is your first step toward self-remembrance. You will slowly become convinced that it is precisely what you cannot see using physical vision that is real, while what you see using physical vision is unreal, illusory. You need to start with this notion, and based on it, you will be able to conduct the investigation of the illusion.

— *What does it mean to create? I can feel my new self based on certain sensations. Here I am, a new human being who has just been born.*

See yourself as an actor playing a role

— Start to see yourself as an actor who was sent here to play a certain role and to become aware of it. Start to observe yourself. I don't know how you will do it. Keep this thought with you all the time. Think about it. You are not what you consider yourself to be. You were sent here. Think about yourself from a side. Observe yourself as you would observe someone else. The more you think about yourself in this way, the more you will feel it. This is the way to fill your new image with energy of feeling. You are a flat rubber ball that needs life to be breathed into it. When you breathe the energy of feelings into this ball, it will come alive. This is what happens during the process of self-investigation. You will understand that this is real, and what you considered to be real, in reality, is unreal. I offer you an opportunity to change the perception of what you consider to be yourself.

Start to investigate this inner girl. At the present time, you cannot see her without tears and pity. She was abused and hurt. Nobody wanted to see her here. Of course, it is better to forget the whole trip, but it is impossible to forget. You say you cannot remember her, but everything that happened to her is written within you in detail. You just blocked it, because these recollections are very painful. You need to review them with the aim to relive them. So, come to the seminars that will help you to review your personal history. Use this opportunity.

You need to have those jolts of energy. In receiving one of them, you will see the knots with which you need to work. You will better understand what you need to do and how to do it. But you can't sleep here. Don't think that someone will work with you and make you feel better. No. You have to

158

constantly carry your own self-investigation. Nobody can do it for you. You need to think about it all the time. This is not something you can do once in a while. I will repeat. You need to listen to the webinars, read books, think and feel like a self-investigator all the time.

It is not easy to become a self-investigator. I started with it today. I showed certain consistent patterns that will lead you to become a self-investigator. I spoke about the fact that you will have serious aggravations in your relationships with family members and people who are close to you as they mirror the opposite sides of the dualities activated by your personality, the dualities that a sleeping man does not want to see in himself. But, as you have not yet investigated the side of duality into which you have started to transfer, for example spirituality, you do not understand what it is. Therefore, that is precisely the situation you need. By increasing the confrontation between the opposite sides of a duality, you accelerate the acquisition of experience. This process will eventually lead you to clearly see both sides of a duality, i.e. to discern them.

The process of acquisition of the experience occurs with a high degree of mechanicality. This is the prerequisite of our lesson. "How great it would be for my husband to listen and to discuss everything with me now. How great it would be if we were to understand everything now," your mind says. But that is not how it will happen. You need people who will resist your spiritual aspirations. They carry this role and you need this role, as spiritual and material are twins that stand back to back looking in opposite directions. You cannot understand one without understanding another.

Investigations of these sides will be of different durations and will occur differently. This is necessary, and this is how it will happen. You cannot avoid it. Nobody can avoid it. It's very important to understand this. You think you can leave your husband or wife who stands in your way, but someone else will show up who will play exactly the same role until you complete the process of accumulation of the necessary experience.

— *Does it mean it is going to get worst?*

— That depends on your point of view. I show you that this is necessary. Is it better or is it worst if it is necessary? In reality, everything is goodness. Everything. There is nothing but goodness, but the conditioned mind does not allow you to see it. It constantly wants to throw something away and to say that if it was not for this, everything would be great. No. It is great now; we just do not understand that it is great. But don't blame yourself for not understanding that this is great. I affirm, everything that happens to you is goodness. When you leave the dual perception, you will see that this is how it is. Everything is goodness. Whatever you experience here is goodness.

By activating a certain duality, you receive an opportunity to interact with two of its opposite sides. In the process, you identify with one side and project another side onto someone else. Therefore, you and another human being represent two sides of the same duality. Now you can understand why I say that others are you, or you and others are one. Now you can understand why, when something appears horrible and ugly to you, causing you to have a strong desire to get rid of it, I call it goodness. It is goodness because the investigation of duality cannot proceed on one, so-called "good" side of polarity. The opposite, so-called "bad" side, should be present. It is similar to a Russian bath-house. After spending some time in a steam room, you jump into a pool of cold water. Is it kaif? Yes, it is kaif! Exactly the same thing happens here. The only difference is that the kaif of the bath house is on the sensory level, while here we are dealing with the kaif of thoughts and feelings.

Self-investigation is always performed by studying duality. One side of duality will always be manifested in other people. You will fight them trying to explain something you do not yet fully understand yourself. They will mirror your own incomprehension, which in the beginning will be enormous. Later, you will find other people who will understand you better, but this understanding will always be incomplete. This will continue until you feel gratitude toward all these people. When you feel this tremendous gratitude to people who played these complicated roles, you will connect the opposite sides of the duality you currently investigate. In particular, your father played one of these roles. He played it mechanically. He was not aware of the role he was playing, but he played it for you. You chose him yourself. When you see this, you will be swept away by this tremendous gratitude to all the people that played these roles, as without them you would have never been able to understand who you are.

— *Now I understand why I destroy men all the time. I understand why I am so harsh. It does not occur on the physical level. I destroy them emotionally. I am very harsh in my relationships with men. I was avenging myself all my life. I thought I was elegant and coquettish. I thought I was virtuous. Now I understand that it was all about revenge.*

— Yes, this is war.

— *I find different ways to attract a man, and when they are close, and I feel that a spider-web is woven, I enjoy them being in my power, and I start to eat them.*

— Exactly. That is what one needs to see.

— And now I understand why I do it. This is what was downloaded—hatred toward men. Being unaware of it, I lose so much. I destroy everything myself.

— Look how sly your game is. A man turned down your girl. You decided to become a stronger man to destroy men. The destroyer in you is this inner man that was formed in you. But he uses female tactics in order to attract and suffocate his victims.

— Yes.

— This is neither bad nor good; this is the way this reality functions. Everyone does it. But the one who considers herself good will not even talk about it. Take a look at the woman who came to the seminar and left the next morning. She left because her game was uncovered.

— Yesterday I tried to correct the situation. I went home and sincerely told my husband that I was killing him. I told him I was a bitch. I enumerated all my negative qualities. He was uneasy. I thought he would get sick.

— When the oppressor openly talks about her oppression, the game is over.

— I was shaking. I was unsure whether I was doing the right thing by telling him everything, but I decided to let myself go. Whatever happens happens. As a result, we talked until two o'clock in a morning. I was talking and talking. He took it all in quietly and stoically. I asked him, "Do you understand that I was killing you? Do you understand I am killing you now, and perhaps will continue to kill you?" And he said, "Haven't you noticed it yourself?" – "I noticed, but I never thought about it. I thought that this was a normal way to behave." It shook my man very hard. I told him I would probably not go back to the seminar. He was very quiet this morning.

— He is trying to figure out how you are going to kill him now.

— And your book is still on our kitchen table. I did not put it away, even though I am done reading it. I told him, "Look, this is how it is. Kill me if you want to. All of this was in me, and now it is out, whether you like it or not. But I am also your mirror. You are in it too." To make a long story short, he thought it was all crazy. Then he took your book and started to read, repeating, "How interesting. How interesting." Then I thought it was crazy.

— Look, everything starts with you. It seems crazy to discuss these things, but then you start talking, and at the same time you observe yourself.

— This was funny, and I was not even drunk.

— His relationship toward you will change, as your relationship toward him starts to change. Stop blaming anybody for what you do not understand. Start talking about what you do not understand. From the point of view commonly accepted here, this might sound crazy. Nobody does it. People will call you crazy. This is precisely what will give you an opportunity to change these relationships. This will give you an opportunity to change the quality of your relationships. You may find a partner self-investigator in him.

— He got somewhat scared.

— Of course he did. Didn't you get scared?

— Yes. I thought, "Let it be the way it is; somehow we will straighten this out." At the end, he got up and said, "You know, I have a strong desire to live." But when I added that we may need to go to seminars this weekend, he said, "Of course. I just started living, and..."

You need to see another human being as your mirror

— Try to understand, this will happen constantly. You will encounter many difficult situations, but this is the only way out of the dead-end of survival. You exit when you stop blaming others and start talking about yourself. By talking about yourself you will see the opposite side of yourself through the one to whom you tell your story. You will encounter unexpected situations. Your conditioned mind will not be able to predict or plan anything. These situations will lead you from darkness to light. He can start screaming at you, and you will suddenly see how you screamed at him before, not understanding it. You will start to untie the knot of your fate. Self-investigation provides an opportunity to untie what appears to be impossible to untie. **Do not blame him. Always talk about yourself.**

— *I have a sensation similar to Vera's. How is it possible? I am leaving for a week, forsaking my family.*

— I forsake my half-strangled husband. Who will strangle him while I am here?

— *The feeling of guilt is still present.*

— Do you feel guilty that you have not finished him off?

— *It is not obvious where the feeling of guilt is coming from.*

— *It is obvious to me. I blamed him before. I used to say, "You do not understand anything. That is not what you think." That's where the feeling of guilt is coming from.*

— The feeling of guilt appears because you hit each other on the weak spots. People who are close know each other very well. When one hits another on a weak spot, the opponent

164

retaliates, reciprocally hitting his partner's weak spot. That's how you show your weak spots to each other. Use it. This is very important. It will not be simple. You can lose awareness. You can get hysterical. You can start screaming or get depressed. Your partners will show you what your manipulation is built on. You hit them. They hit back, and what hurts you the most is what their manipulation is built upon. However, your own manipulation is built on the same thing.

— *I asked myself what was it that I wanted to see? Why did I come here? What did I want to hear today? I could not answer this question. Everything was blurry. I did not understand anything. But, as soon as people started to talk, my situation, the situation I walked in here with this morning but completely forgot on arrival, was discussed by other people. The second speaker was talking about my situation. As a result of your dialogue, I understood how painful her relationship with her father was. I cried. I cried thinking that I was not needed. It was a terrible shock for me to feel that my parents did not need me. I understand now how strongly identified I was. Now I hear that and internally I am with her, but it does not touch me as strongly as …*

— As the one to whom it is connected.

— *It does not touch me as it would touch someone who was badly hurt by people, as it would touch someone who was almost killed emotionally and physically. However, I think I start to feel gratitude toward my parents, as it is precisely because of these situations that I am who I am—the one who sits here.*

— What sits here is a tendency to acquire experience. Please, understand that you as personality are your experience. Personality is created in order to acquire a certain experience and move to another experience. In the illusion of sleep, the transfer to another experience or to another personality occurs only through so-called death, which by itself is an illusion. You

165

will not die, you will change. Death is just a change of decorations. Our process offers the fastest way to acquire experience—awareness. And we don't need to drop our physical bodies here. We don't need to die physically.

But we are not what we consider ourselves to be. If you think you are the girl your parents did not want here, you are mistaken. If you think you are the woman that thinks about the girl that her parents did not want, you are mistaken. But this needs to be lived through, needs to be experienced. This is the experience you came here for. And yes, this was the way you acquired it, and this is precisely the experience you need. But you can only receive this experience by having the notions of yourself that you have, being identified with the images that were created specifically in order to acquire this experience. In reality, we are the experience that is eternally perfect and becomes aware of itself.

— *I am sitting here quietly while there is a war inside: to say or not to say? Yesterday I saw Lilia massaging Pint. I thought to myself, "I want to massage him too." But another voice inside me said, "Here is your man next to you, do what you want." Okay, I think, I am descending to lower chakras again. I straightened myself up and started to talk to someone. Everything was running smoothly for a while, when suddenly I look at them again and saw Lilia sitting on his lap.*

— Are you jealous?

— *Well …*

— Are you jealous or not?

— *Yesterday I felt I was not.*

— You are lying.

— *Help me to sort it out.*

— You are like a kettle with constantly boiling water. A woman approaches me and you get instantly jealous.

— *Well, I have to exit this state somehow.*

— You cannot exit out of anything until you become aware of what you feel, think, and do. You cannot exit out of this until you say to yourself, "I am jealous."

— *That is what I say.*

— No, you do not say that. You constantly discuss different stories that get you jealous, but you never say, "I am jealous."

— *Okay, I am jealous. Now what?*

— Nothing. You have just stated a fact. Everything else was a prelude to it.

— ***Is jealousy a vibration of low frequency?***

— **It is a vibration of lower frequency we all happen to occupy. This is why I do not call it shit the way you do. Until you feel these vibrations thoroughly, you cannot transform them. How can you transform something that you do not see? If you are jealous, say it. Say, "I am jealous" and start seeing it. Only then will transformation start. Otherwise, nothing will be transformed. But you do not want to acknowledge that. Until you see what it is the way it is, you will not be able to do anything with it. Until you see yourself getting jealous, blaming, and killing others, you will not be able to do anything about it. You will do it mechanically. It is inevitable.**

— *I want to say something in regards to this. I listened to you, and I saw everything around me from the point of view of the relationship "husband—wife." I was married four times. I lived with my first husband for a week, with the second one for four years, with the third one for thirteen years, and I have been with my fourth husband for twenty years now. But I always thought I was great and they were bad. I always looked for someone better. Being here I understood the uselessness of this search. I will not be able to live with another man either. I also understood that I am killing another human being.*

167

— We all do.

— *I do it quite forcefully. I manipulate him very well.*

— Yes. **There is nothing beside this in the old matrix of consciousness. We need to become aware that everything we call "love" is war.**

— *I tell her right things. I invite her to start a family business—she declines. Her health deteriorates. All the tests return normal, and she appears healthy, but at the same time she is apathetic and does not want to live. And I am the one to blame.*

— Right. Everyone manipulates and everyone uses his own tactics.

— *I see how she manipulates me.*

— Now you need to see how you manipulate her.

— *I am trying to sort it out.*

Look for awareness—everything else will follow

— Until you see it, you will not be able to change. It is impossible to change what you do not see. Seeing is action. Everyone comes here asking, "How can I do it?" And I say, "Seeing is action." Look for awareness—everything else will follow. When you see something clearly, you will not be able to do it the old way. That is why seeing is action. You can whirl with dervishes, read mantras, but nothing will happen because you do not see what is the way it is.

— *She says that until I started to study here everything was normal.*

— She is irritated by your spirituality.

— *It does not bother me. Well, actually, I suffer.*

— Everyone suffers here. You will continue to suffer for as long as the dualities of your personality, dualities you are not even aware of, are activated. And the stronger these dualities are activated, the heavier your suffering will be. This strong activation of dualities is a necessary experience. This experience is being acquired here only through suffering. You can't get it any other way. Suffering can be diminished and transformed into empathy through awareness, but the phase of acquisition of experience has to be endured. Everyone carries dualities that needed to be activated and taken apart. You cannot see them clearly unless you pull them in opposite directions. **The main principle of our process is to pull a duality apart in order to see it better, to see it as one scale, and to connect.**

— *I usually arrange things neatly. Even in your books, I managed to find justification for myself—I don't need to look anywhere but inside, so I look inside.*

— **Start seeing the duality to which your worst suffering is connected. You are masturbating mentally. You need to activate and strengthen this duality. Then it will start to develop. For example, if you say you are smart, some idiot will show up. He will trick you and cause you to suffer. If you insist you are handsome, an ugly man will outdo you in a love affair.**

You don't see your dualities yet. Create an intention to see them, and you will start to see them, and their polarities.

Walk into your suffering consciously. This is the accelerated way of spiritual development. **Declare your intent to become aware of your dualities.** You need to have intent. How this will happen is not known, but when the intention is declared, it starts to realize itself. Only then will you be able to distinguish the dualities of your personality and their polar sides.

169

— Can I please talk through my state? Very strong sensations are passing through me. I want to run away. I feel I am going to burst. Quite frequently, I want to palliate these feelings and sensations by eating. I started to think that I want to buy yogurt at the store next door. At first, I concentrated on the desire to run there fast. Then, I saw my desire to leave, if even for a couple of minutes. Now it is followed by a heavy physical sensation. I feel enormous pressure. I am ready to burst. I wanted to talk this through in order to understand what it is.

— Give birth. What do you want to give birth to? What is asking to be delivered? What is it? Talk!

— No thoughts…nothing concrete … just a certain state.

— The state is connected to the activation of certain dualities. I am emphasizing this again. I amplify their internal opposition. You are aware of them on the physical and sensory level, but you cannot define them mentally yet.

— I have a strongly expressed duality of being here with all my soul and body. The second part, probably material, does not want to be here. It wants to relax.

— We can call this duality: "to wake up—to continue to sleep." I do not allow you to sleep here. That is why you want to run away from here and to fall asleep for a couple of minutes. You want to forget everything.

— One stops perceiving and it appears that one side says, "Get out of here." But another part says, "Stay here, feel, sense, and experience." The first side says, "Okay, let yourself relax a bit" – "No, stay, experience."

— That is the duality "To sleep—To wake up." This is the main duality that will be shaken up here. It is similar to a man who has not slept for many days. He is barely able to sit up in a chair. People shake him up. They don't allow him to sleep.

170

They lift and drag him somewhere. They pinch him. He is falling. He is about to lose consciousness.

— *This is more than one can physically withstand.*

— *I came here in such a state of malaise and body ache. I am asleep, and I need to awaken. I came here, and my body is aching now.*

— What does "body ache" means? We discussed the fact that body is made out of cells, and cells represent consciousness of a certain level. The vibration that passes through here starts to change the molecular composition of these cells and increase the vibration of their consciousness. That is why you have these bad aches. You are aching precisely in the places where cells have the lowest vibrations. The level of vibrations during seminars is very high.

— *I spoke to a woman who came to investigate the concept of "Holistic Psychology." She is interested because her occupation is connected with the upbringing of girls and she wanted to see how it could affect their spirituality.*

— She is running an institute for grande dames?

— *When we were hitting each other on the face yesterday, she showed a lot of aggression. She was highly animated afterwards. She said, "Just imagine what I would tell my girls." At the end, she called us a cult, and said she could not understand what we were doing.*

— *She has also said that she has both positive and negative sides swinging back and forth. She said she was fully harmonized and did not need to be here. So, in order not to destroy this harmony she left.*

— Take a look at how illusion reacts to reality. When a man gets into an atmosphere where reality is being discussed, he starts to grab for the illusion. He has to be able to tutor others. He insists everything is great with him, others have problems. When he is stimulated to see his own problems, he gets confused and irritated. He calls us a cult and runs away screaming.

171

— I read some old letters today. In reading them, I felt I wrote all of them myself, even though these letters were from different people. They all carried a common theme: separation and self-destruction.

— Yes, this is the main theme of a drama theater called "Earth." When you are ready to see it, you will see it. On the other hand, you can create an illusion that you see it already, everything is great with you, and fall asleep without being awaken. That is a typical behavior of the one who is asleep. In order to see things the way they are, one has to have courage, real courage. To see your own weakness is courage.

— Prior to this seminar a thought popped into my head that appeared to be totally crazy to me. It looks like on a subconscious level I try to destroy myself or, at least, age as fast as possible. In reality, I don't feel my age, but at the same time I do everything so my body will age faster. In this way, I can destroy myself or feel my age and come to terms with it.

— This is a fast way to die.

— *I don't understand what I am striving for.*

— Remember we spoke of optimal solution. I ask you earlier what the facts of this reality are. These two facts are birth and death. So, the optimal solution for all life problems is death. The mind works using the optimal program. Therefore, one needs to die optimally. In your case, you need to age in order to die.

— And as fast as possible.

— Another man's optimal decision is to die from a bullet. He goes to war. Everyone chooses his own way.

— You mean whatever we do is always optimal?

— Yes, from the point of view of the conditioned mind that has a certain program, it does everything optimally.

Disease is a result of your condemnation of yourself

— I just started to understand something about my physical body. I came here from St. Petersburg. I got in a car, and I felt something in my spine. Yesterday, I went to bed, and I felt this pain in my lower back again. I could not lie on my side. Now I am okay. Pain is gone.

— What we call a disease here is a result of self-destruction. What is a common approach to disease? Nobody tells us that we destroy ourselves. We go to a doctor, and we are told we have a certain disease. It just appears. I got a cold. Someone sneezed at me. I fell. I got into an accident. Someone rear-ended me. And a doctor prescribes you a medication. This is a low vibrational approach. A high vibration approach presupposes seeing how I created this disease and how I maintain it. How do I create this particular self-destruction?

I assert, our diseases are the results of our condemnation of ourselves. These condemnations are directed toward different organs. These situations need to be carefully sorted out. If I condemn myself for not being grounded, I will hurt my feet or they may start hurting on their own. If I cannot get what I want, my hands will show it by becoming arthritic, or by getting some other disease. All our organs are functional. Condemnation of a certain function leads to disease of a certain organ. If I blame the world for the absence of love, breast cancer or myocardial infarction may develop. If I blame myself for sexuality, I could create a disease of the sexual organs. For example, I can create ovarian or uterine cancer. By the way, all sexually transmitted diseases are connected to the blame directed to one's sexuality.

173

— But one side constantly blames another.

— Yes. The illusion of separation that is accepted for reality here gives birth to a dramatic show the essence of which is blame, condemnation, and guilt. You will find blame, condemnation, and guilt everywhere.

The oppressor blames, while the victim feels self-pity. But in reality, the oppressor also blames himself. The victim feels self-pity, but the victim also blames herself through this oppressor. All of these roles are inside a human being, who blames and feels guilty at the same time.

— So, what does one to do when both parts are blaming each other?

— You need to understand that these parts are in you.

— Yes, they are in me. I cannot separate them.

— What do you mean, you cannot separate them? It will be correct to say, "I cannot unite them."

— Neither this, nor that...

— Wait a minute, if I am already separated, how can I be unable to separate?

— But two of them are present in one body.

— Yes, that is why we need to sort out what state you are in right now. I am pushing you toward it all the time. I am talking about it constantly so you start to understand it. Leaning on the new notions, you can transform the old notions. To start with, you should see that you have opposite parts that fight each other inside you. These parts make up your personality, and because you think that you are your personality, you fight yourself. Transformation occurs as one becomes aware of this fight of dualities of one's own personality. That is what we work with.

I explained how your personality is structured. It is extremely difficult to understand, but I will continue to return to this topic as the knowledge of dual nature of our personal perception is the foundation of our work. It needs to be reviewed again and again as it shows itself everywhere and in everything that surrounds you, but most importantly in you. This is your life.

— *Is the condemnation of sexuality caused by morality? For example, when I condemn sexuality, I am highly moral.*

— Yes, you are a noble woman that grew out of noble girl.

— *And at the same time, this noble woman oppresses men. She lures them in and then enjoys the situation when they are by her feet. At the same time she is highly moral. She suppresses her own sexuality, and as a result she gets a gynecological disease.*

— Yes.

— *I was so good at it. I lost my uterus, and now I can see the mechanism of my own creation.*

— *For the last few days, my liver was in distress. I just recalled that I was sick with hepatitis in the army. I experienced myself as a victim there, and I was blaming others. "Oppressor—victim." For the last three days, I experienced the same states, and I saw how I oppress myself with awareness.*

— Oppression by awareness becomes a reality when you are not aware of something in yourself and use awareness as a concept to oppress someone. In order to be tough and good, you need to operate out of notion, "Jesus loves us all, but you bastard do not want to pray to him." This is a notion with which you can oppress. There a many other notions. Awareness is not something you can use to oppress. Awareness is not a notion. You cannot make an instrument of oppression out of it. But you can create a notion of awareness and use it to oppress others. So, if you oppress by awareness, it means you do not understand what awareness is.

Awareness is what sees everything without judgment or blame. When you are aware, you start seeing everything the way it is without blame. I repeat, awareness is not a notion. Awareness is what clearly sees everything that exists in three dimensional reality, precisely because it is not of it. How can you oppress something that does not exist here? That is why in order to oppress with awareness you need to transform it into some kind of notion. But then it is not awareness any longer. I doubt you clearly understand what I am saying now, but nevertheless, I am going to repeat myself again and again, and maybe it would provide you with a necessary push.

Some may call what I discuss here a notion, and some may say that I oppress you with this notion. Nothing of the sort. The main theme here is awareness, and awareness is not a notion. That is why I can change my notions very easily. I simply use them until they are useful for a given human being. Later, I change them. I am not fixated on anything. I am not in a closed circle. Awareness is something that sees everything that exists the way it is. You cannot say anything about it, but you can enter it and see what is the way it is. But then you will talk about what is as it is.

You cannot talk about what awareness is. Being aware, you can observe the images you consider to be yourself. By observing these images, you change them and now observe the changes that occur. Your conditioned mind sees you as a compilation of certain images, beliefs, and convictions. In reality, this is just a snapshot of you taken at a certain moment from a certain position.

Awareness is a high quality camera that constantly makes snapshots of your mental, emotional, physical, and behavioral states from multiple positions. The one who wants to play the "oppressor—victim" game will try to convert this camera to a knife and to pock others with it.

— *That's what I was doing after the last seminar.*

— In this case, "awareness" turns into a new weapon you try to use to oppress others. In reality, awareness is not a weapon and cannot be used in order to fight. You can transform it into one of your conceptions, but I repeat again and again, that is totally opposite of what I try to explain. When you say something about holistic psychology, understand that this is your own vision, not mine. Everyone here talks for himself. That is why there are no diplomas here. Many ask for diplomas. They want to graduate from a school of holistic psychology and to carry eternal good to the world. I tell them, "No. If you want to lead people behind you, use your own name, please."

— *I noticed another important thing that concerns knowledge. We frequently apply knowledge and intellect harshly. If knowledge is not felt through the heart, there is no awareness. One is identified, and there is no opportunity to see what is the way it is.*

Psychoanalysis and psychosynthesis

— Awareness comes through experience. Awareness can be seen as the fusion of the old knowledge with new experience. You can only do it by yourself and only in relationship to yourself. Others serve you as mirrors, helping you to see in them what is related to you. **As soon as I start to blame someone, I am off the correct course.**

— *I previously thought that awareness is present when you see the situation, sort it out, and analize it.*

— See the situation created by you.

— *Yes, I mean you see the situation, and you can describe how you created it. Alex is doing it all the time. He is a psychotherapist who can sort out any situation.*

— What is psychoanalysis? What is analysis? Analysis is partition. And what is synthesis? It is unification. Psychoanalysis is one side, and psychosynthesis is another side. Every other psychologist is a psychoanalyst, but I have not seen many psychologists practicing psychosynthesis. Psychoanalysis should go together with psychosynthesis. Connection can only come through the heart, as intellect is the apparatus for shredding. It will shred everything given to it and ask for more. You will give birth to many fragments during analysis. How can you connect them?

From the psychoanalysis point of view, the more you are shredded up, the better you are, and the better and grander your psychoanalyst is. But how are we to connect these shredded fragments of yours? We don't know. So, please, get your analysis and synthesis together. Divide in order to see, and see in order to unite. What is the formula I constantly discuss? I discuss something that appears to be analysis, but it is not. Let's call it discernment. There is a big difference between analysis and discernment. Discernment does not crush something that is whole to pieces. It helps to clearly see the opposite sides of duality. I discern two sides of duality.

— *It depends on the state one is in. One can say the correct words while being in a state of lower vibrations.*

— *So, out of which state do you listen now?*

— Look, you are blaming again. You are constantly rolling down into blame.

— *I do not blame him now. Well, I blame myself. It means both him and myself.*

— You specialize in intellectually subtle blame. You do it well. Moreover, one can think that you are not blaming but analyzing. "Let me analyze you." At one point, a man will arrive into your life, and you will come to him and say, "Let me analyze you dear." And he will reply, "Yes, dear. Please, analyze me." That will be the summit of your love. That is how your love rendezvous would run. Unconditional love is synthesis. It is the connection and the summit of all feelings. Analysis is what being left after all the feelings have been dried up. During a chemical reaction some ingredients precipitate as dry residuals. That is what analysis is. It is a dry residual.

If you want to decrease water vibrations, you need to freeze it. If you want to increase water vibrations, you need to warm it up. Then it will turn into vapor. You are discussing a dry residual. You keep talking and talking about it. I return it to you. That is my main function: to return to you what you express and to describe it to you. When you see it from a side, an opportunity for transformation appears. You are producing dry residual in great quantities. If you want to receive higher quality fractions, you need to start the synthesis of your feelings.

Please, briefly describe your current states.

Indeterminate state

— *I am currently in a state of being aware of the process.*

— Please, talk about your feelings.

— *I am still dead.*

— *I am vibrating inside. Everything vibrates and shakes. My body is in a state of tension. It trembles.*

— Are those serious shakes?

— *Very serious. It may not be seen from the outside, but inside it feels as a constant and very strong vibration. I don't know what it is.*

— I. Who is this I?

— *It eased up.*

— *I still sense a vibration.*

179

— "Vibration" is a mental definition of what?

— *Well, shake. I dont know how to define it better.*

— Those are physical sensations. How about feelings?

— *It's a happy state. I experience an awakened state. In such a state, problems are being solved. I frequently find myself asleep.*

— Who finds himself asleep?

— *Probably the one who also used to wake up at certain times.*

— I found myself asleep. Does it mean I woke up?

— *Yes, but one immediately become aware that one was asleep for a long time.*

— This is a good indicator of an incipient awareness. "Opa! I am asleep!"

— *A state of such … internal sensation ... one can call it.*

— Do you mean gut?

— *Tears without pity. These tears provide a relief. Something is getting cleansed inside. And now I sense lightness everywhere.*

— Where? Do you sense it at the level of your bra or at the level of your underwear? Don't you know what chakras are?

— *What chakra is there?*

— Okay, let's not go into chakras. Just say, "I feel vibration at the level of my bra. At the level of my glasses, I feel prickling."

— *I am just curious. I feel myself in the role of a spectator. You are all united by some idea, some aim, and I observe. I am very excited. It is very interesting.*

— Later, it will be very not interesting.

— *I don't know yet.*

— But I know already.

— *I understood that if I were to get into all of this, it would be very difficult. I did not get half of what you have said.*

— And you will not get it, because you just listen while this needs to be lived through, experienced.

— *It depends on what one came here with. I did not come to solve global problems. I came to simply feel the emptiness of life.*

— Take a look at this "simply." Is not your main problem the emptiness of life?

— *Everything is normal in my case. I have a normal husband and normal kids.*

— Here walks a normal little girl, and here she is a normal young married woman, and now she is normal grandmother, and then grandmother dies. That is it. Is that your show?

— *It is difficult.*

— It is extremely difficult unless you experience it in full awareness.

— *Tatiana verbalizes all my thoughts.*

— Have you chosen to stay in our show through her?

— *I just see how difficult it is for her.*

— And who is it easy for here? Except, of course, you. In your case everything is normal.

— *It does not mean I am not going to join in. I observe. I try to understand something.*

— I would be so alive if I was not so dead. Is that so?

— *I am in a state of internal opening. Shock, observation, shock.*

— *On the level of underwear, I want to use a bathroom. On the level of the bra, I feel excitation and peace. On the level of the forehead, I know that I don't know anything.*

— *Excitement in the body, legs, and arms.*

— *A state of awakening. I sense that my legs are tired and ready to be dropped.*

— At the level of the pants, my hands get sweaty, and at the level of my socks, my eyes tear. I am a Zen master accepting my fifth initiation.

— *I have a sensation of depression at the level of underwear.*

— How so?

— *A state of constriction.*

— Constriction at the level of underwear? A man can say, "I experience a high elevation at the level of my underwear, seeing depression at the level of your panties. I feel spiritual ascension at the level of underwear. I get higher, and harder."

— *I am in a state of excitement similar to what others described, at the level of the bra. I feel trembling inside. It is extremely difficult to talk.*

— *I am laughing. My jaw is hurting. I sense everything other people describe and they help me to open up.*

— *I don't know where each of my levels work, but inside of me there is a creature that slowly but surely is getting ready to experiment. I am not sure what it is, but I like it.*

— Are you ready for reckless experiments?

— *Yes.*

— *I am shaking. My knee hurts. My head is empty—no thoughts.*

— *I feel strong impatience and excitement.*

— This something, somewhere, and somehow will surely, possibly happen to you sometimes.

CHAPTER 4

VICTIM LOOKS FOR AN OPPRESSOR

•◆•

I like what I do not like

— Who is going to start today?

— *I looked at what I like and what I dislike. Then I switched. I looked at what I don't like and what I like. One I like, another I don't like. Looking at what I dislike, I felt, I like it. Looking at what I like, I felt I don't like it. Then I felt what I "like—don't like," simultaneously seeing what I "don't like—like." Now there is no more separate "like" and "don't like," but "like—don't like" as one whole. However, there is something I don't understand. I see my own thoughts and feelings. That I like. Externally this is called Dennis, and as much as I like to feel it, it torments me.*

— Are you talking about someone real who you like?

— *Yes, I like him.*

— And what do you like about him?

— *I like the feeling of harmony I experience thinking about him.*

— You like the feeling of harmony that appears in you in connection with him.

183

— *Yes.*

— So, you identify with him and feel harmony.

— *This feeling of harmony also torments me.*

— A feeling of harmony cannot cause torment. Therefore, this is not harmony. This is something else.

— *Perhaps, I feel this torment because of his absence?*

— So, there is no torment when he is present?

— *There is torment.*

— When he is present, there is also torment?

— *Yes, but there is also a state of harmony.*

— And is there torment when he is absent?

— *There is torment, but then the state of harmony is absent.*

— So, the torment is present in both cases?

— *Yes.*

— So, what is your question?

— *The question is if it is inside, it is also outside, but I don't see him outside. I experience a feeling toward him, touching him with my thought.*

— Outside is what is inside.

— *I feel it without seeing him.*

— So, what is the question? Do I want to see him or do I want to feel? What is the question?

— *I want to see. But this is not my choice. This is my "want."*

— Why do I want to see him?

— *I want to be with him.*

— Why do I want to be with him?

— *I want to experience certain states.*

— What kind of states?

— *A state of happiness because he exists.*

— If he is to disappear, there would not be happiness?

— *He is absent, but feelings and thoughts about him are present.*

— Okay. How is he different from others?

— *I like him mentally, emotionally, and physically.*

— So, he calls up certain feelings in you, feelings that you like.

— *Yes.*

— Okay. Do you feel these feelings in yourself only in connection with him? Do they appear in you in his absence?

— *I feel them very sharply in connection to him.*

— What is it exactly in him that causes these feelings in you?

— *His appearance. His shape. I like his body, his voice, and his words.*

— How so? What can you tell us about him?

— *He is "timid—courageous," "handsome—ugly," "pleasant—unpleasant."*

— *It seems to me you confuse yourself when you use these dualities.*

— So, you see yourself in him.

— *Yes. I feel like a woman with him. Usually, I also feel like a man, but with him I am a woman only.*

— So, he allows you to clearly discern between your inner man and your inner woman.

— *Yes.*

— Do other men offer you this opportunity?

— *They do.*

— But if you talk about him all the time, perhaps others allow it less or do not allow it?

— *Other men allow it less.*

— Why do other men allow you to experience your inner woman less? Take one man who does not allow you to experience your inner woman at all.

— *I am all mixed up. Does not allow me to do what?*

— Take a man who does not allow you to feel your inner man and your inner woman. How do other men differ from

185

him? I am helping you to make this discernment. In order for you to understand, you need to be able to discern. Here is this man you have been talking about, and this is the way he is. There is someone else who is different from him. What is the difference between them? Why do you experience this state with him, and do not experience it with other men? I am asking you to go and to experience it with other men. I am trying to help you to discern your states.

— *When I see him, I feel these feelings.*

— So, when you see him you see your man, and in such a way you start to identify with your woman. Do I understand you correctly?

— *Yes.*

— This happens better with him than with any other man.

— *Yes.*

— At other times, you feel a man inside who has the qualities of an oppressor.

— *Yes.*

— So, everything is inside of you. The parts we are currently discussing are inside you. When you meet people, certain parts of your personality get activated. Some parts get activated in connection to so-called positive feelings, while other parts get activated in connection to so-called negative feelings. Other people simply cause you to manifest certain notions of yours about yourself. Am I correct?

— *Yes.*

— So, what is the question? Is there a question, or do you just want to share this?

— *It seems to me that this inner man is me. You have already said that.*

— This is a part of your inner man that is manifested physically. Seeing him outside, you become aware of your feminine part.

— *And that tortures me.*

— What exactly *tortures* you?

— *Him not being here. I have this feeling inside me, but he is not here.*

— But you experience this state irrespective of whether he is physically present or not. He provides you with an opportunity to feel it. But in reality, he is you. So, his absence does not deprive you of this experience. It is in you. Yes, in his physical presence you can feel and see it easier. In his absence, it gets blurry.

— *Yes, it gets a bit blurry, but it is good.*

— So, what is the question? Have you figured something out?

— *I did not feel it through.*

— You started to tell us this story for a reason. I am asking you two questions. Why did you tell us this story? Did you receive what you wanted to receive?

— *It looks like I just wanted to share.*

— But we share for a reason. We share in order to manifest, to figure out, and to see something clearly. There should be some kind of a result. I am asking you again. Did you receive a result?

— *No, there is no result.*

— Then why did you do it? In reality, there is a result, but you don't see it.

— *I don't see a result.*

— Because you do not have an inquiry. Without inquiry, there will be no answer. So, do you want to have an answer or not? You said something was tormenting you. Are you satisfied with it? I don't understand what satisfies you and what does not. Actually, this is the tendency of your personality. You try something without understanding why and what for. But you constantly try something. You do something, but you don't say anything about it. That's what happens with you all the time.

How ego proves its toughness

— Listening to Lilia, I saw myself. When I was working on my Ph.D. in literature, I constantly had a desire to show how smart I was and to play with words in conversations with people, as I was studying semantics, the meaning of words. I recalled those times when I was so absorbed by forms that it was extremely important for me just to talk, just to pronounce something. From the standpoint of linguistics, Lilia's mentioning dualities is a very nice trick. I had a sensation that I would have said it myself in order to play with words: to say something just in order to say it.

— What is important here is not to say something but to become aware of the dual notions of your conditioned mind. Then you can play with them. If you are not aware of them— they play you. You call it a "play," but it is not obvious what you are playing with, and what kind of game you are playing.

— I know that I can do it. I talk this way when I am with people that cannot do it.

— So, you are showing your superiority.

— Yes.

— Superiority appears in connection with something. You have to have a ground for superiority. For example, two tough guys stand in front of each other. How can you understand who is tougher?

— Are we talking about parameters of superiority?

188

— Yes. You play well with words, but you cannot lift a heavy dumbbell. Some bodybuilder will come in, lift a dumbbell, and call you a looser.

— *Is this a question of power?*

— This is a question of "Who is smarter?" You stay next to a bodybuilder. He is lifting weights and you are playing with words—you scorn each other.

— *Horrible.*

— We are returning to the eternal question of pride again. Pride gets born out of something. It is not born out of nothing. Everyone is proud of something. Moreover, people can invent anything in order to have their pride. Book of Guinness, for example, contains records of competition between spitters. I can spit thirty feet, and your spit can't even reach a five feet mark. Here is pride. I can fart "Besame Mucho," and you can't. One can find a reason for pride in anything. My ears are small and yours are big.

So, one can be proud of anything. An invalid can be proud of having thirty ulcers on his legs. Pride can be created out of anything. People occupy themselves with pride all the time. Everyone is proud of something. You cannot get rid of pride unless you understand how it is created.

Personality identifies itself based on certain qualities. We discussed some of these qualities, and we can find many more. All of them are dual. Personality identifies itself with one side of a certain quality. Then, opposing itself to the opposite side of this quality, it creates its pride. In this game of ascent and descent, you raise one side of a duality and drop another side. This is how pride is created. This is a see-saw. Someone descends, and you ascend. The lower the opponent descends, the higher you rise. In reality, you and your opponent are one, but no one sees it. The higher I rise, the lower my opponent falls. I scream to him, "Hey looser, take a look at how high I am." I swell up with pride. But pretty soon my side of the see-saw comes down, and I get to be in the same state my opponent experienced being on the bottom. Here, I experience suffering. That is the mechanism of creation of suffering. If you intend to exit it, you have to see this mechanism. You experience pride in playing with words (at this point we have not figured out what exactly it is). This pride will be the reason for you to experience humiliation, when you flip to the opposite side.

— *It happened already.*

— Of course it did, and many times.

— *It happened few years ago. For three years I could not say a word. I could not say anything. I could not understand what was happening to me. Friends would say, "Tell us Violette, tell us..." I could not say anything. I felt like a complete idiot.*

— Idiot man or idiot woman?

— Idiot man.

— So, first you felt yourself to be a smart man, and then you felt like an idiot. You display quite a strong male side. The mind represents the masculine side. Everyone, please take a look at this woman here. She calls herself Violette, but in reality she is a man. She is also a woman, but currently her masculine side is talking logic. And she can't understand how such an amazingly smart linguist is unable to connect two words. Your transfer to the opposite state is linked to someone who now ascends to the place you previously occupied. You have spoken about marriage. Your husband probably took the spot you used to occupy.

— *Which I used to occupy?*

— Which you used to occupy. And that starts to torture you. This is a fight between two men: your inner man and your husband.

— *If he was a man...*

— He was not a man?

— *I am just thinking out loud. I have not thought about it this way before.*

— You have never thought whether your husband was a man or not? Who is a man and who is a woman in your house?

Whose model of behavior did you accept in childhood?

— The question is which model of behavior was accepted by you during childhood. We receive a personal program from our parents: mother and father. But it is more complicated than that. It is not known whether mother was mother. She could have been a father. It is also not known whether father was father. He could have been mother. This is a question. There are two models of behavior: masculine and feminine. A child picks up a model of behavior of a winner. A child may resist the father who punishes him frequently, but nevertheless internally feel that father's model of behavior is a winning model. One becomes what one fights.

You absorb and incorporate as conscious the model of behavior of a parent with whom you have had more conflicts growing up. The program uploads through emotional conflicts. The more emotional these conflicts were, the stronger the program is fixated in you. Which parent did you have more emotional conflicts with growing up?

— *I had more conflicts with my mother.*

— Was your mother displayed by a woman or by a man?

— *With my mother…*

— Was she a man?

— *Yes, my mother was a man. I used to say to myself that I will never be like her.*

— That's how the upload of a program starts: "I will never be like her." All the conflicts between parents and kids start with this fatal phrase: "I will never be such and such …" And then you become exactly that.

— *Yes.*

— So, your mother realized the male model. We are living in a patriarchal world that is built on male logic. Our society is built by men. We can see how wonderful it is. Scientific progress advances. This is what people call evolution. A few years ago, we were shooting arrows, and now we are dropping atomic bombs. If you want to reach so-called success in a patriarchal world—and everyone is brought up here to strive for success—you have to be better than others. So, people elbow each other in order to be better. Career, power, and money are being praised here. So, certain logic arises based on these values. It is a conditioned logic. Effective business strategies are built. This is a patriarchal world. The successful model of behavior in the patriarchal world is connected to male logic and oppression. Let's take a look at culture. What do theaters, movies, and music carry?

— *Emotions.*

— What kind of emotions? For example, a group called "Viagra" comes on stage. Have you seen this group?

— *I have seen them.*

— Take a look at TV shows: "Sopranos," "Bachelor," "The Apprentice." What do these shows offer? Can this culture uplift the vibrations of feelings? Is it so important to elbow every other competitor in order to become a "star"? This is what patriarchal society is built upon. A child starts to perceive the logic of patriarchy because it is presented here as the logic of winners. That is why we see women who behave as men. Have you noticed this?

— *I did. A man can do anything, but a woman cannot. A woman always owes something.*

— Whatever is in demand here gets developed.

— *Man is free.*

— What do you mean "man is free"? When and where is he free? He is free to create an atomic bomb, to start a fight or a war. Is that freedom? He is free to shoot everyone and to get behind the bars or to be killed? Where else is he free?

— *He is free to choose his own fear.*

Freedom is an opportunity to choose that which does not exist here

— There is no freedom where fear is present. A mechanical man can have no freedom. The notion of freedom is a grand illusion that is being cultivated here. Democratic society is a jail from which nobody even tries to break away, as no one thinks there is anything better. This is a sophisticated jail without walls. What kind of freedom can a mechanical man have? Freedom is an opportunity to have a choice. What kind of choice do you have here? A human being receives something from the start and stays in it, where is freedom? Remember the times of socialism: "Choose the secretary general!" What do you mean—choose? There is only one secretary general.

— *This is exactly how it is done in a democratic society, with the only exception that there are two secretary generals.*

— That is exactly what I am saying. A democratic society is a highly sophisticated illusion of a freedom of choice. That is why by body you are a woman, but the model of behavior you use is masculine. What is feminine? It is something crying, grieving, and hitting her head on the wall screaming: "Why did you leave me?" But in order to do that, you need to kill the one who left you. Only then this great dramatic scene of a woman's life can be played out.

— *We laugh, but I observed women who surround me at work, and I noticed how masculine they are. They lack soft femininity that would inspire and give strength to a man.*

— Correct. Human civilization is "evolving." We are sorting out the way it "evolves." Where is the feminist movement coming from?

— *It comes from the masculine.*

— Yes. Feminists are men in female bodies. They conduct the politics of men. Women unite!

— *Men in women bodies unite.*

— Men in women bodies unite against men in the bodies of men. They like to talk about real men disappearing. There are no real men—only gay men. By the way, a prostitute in a female body receives significantly less than a prostitute in a body of a man. Feminists are men in women bodies. They unite on the basis of physical sex characteristics but carry their male politics through these bodies. These men in women's bodies fight those who are in male bodies. They say, "Let's unite and fight for our freedom together." This is the same fight that patriarchal society stimulates. By the way, what do feminists do when they don't fight for their rights?

— *They create the conception of a fight.*

— I think they are lesbians.

— *I think this is a very important question. I remember my wives. They were men. I ask myself, "Why?" Is it because I manifested primarily as a woman?*

— Your feminine side was activated during these marriages. Your masculine side was represented by your wives.

— *My inner woman was never realized. I understand it now.*

— What do you mean? You just spoke about the woman being present in you? "Man—woman" is a duality. This duality is present in every body. But which side of this duality is being consciously manifested in your body? Which model is taken by you as a model of a winner? Is it a male or female model? I will tell you that people with an underdeveloped feminine side do not get into our process.

— *It seems to me, I am a man. Why do I attract men?*

— There is always a balance. If your feminine side is activated, whether you want it or not, you will attract a masculine side. As you are not a homosexual, you will attract this masculine side, but in a female body.

— *This is not clear.*

— There is a feminine and masculine side in every human being. Our process helps you to integrate these two opposite sides. On the lowest levels of vibrations, the relationship between a man and a woman is always a fight. It is a relationship between the heart and the mind. **Awareness is the highest level of development of the mind, while unconditional love is the highest level of development of the heart.** It is impossible to walk to yourself using one side of the street only; both sides have to be connected. But in order

195

to see what happens in me, I need to start seeing what level of vibrations I happen to occupy now.

You will attract your own parts of which you are not aware. Actually, not only are you unaware of them, you are not even conscious of them. Your level of consciousness is what you see. For example, you are conscious of the fact that you elevate your arm. You are conscious of the fact that you put on a pair of pants. You are conscious of the fact that you have just eaten a burger. But you can also do something of which you are not conscious. Asked later whether you did it or not, you reply, "No I did not." You do not remember it.

The peculiarities of the training ground "Earth"

— Awareness is an opportunity to see what I am conscious of and what I am not conscious of, i.e. to see the creativity of two opposite directors of my "life" show. A human being attracts those parts of himself of which he is not conscious. Then these parts start to interact. Everything that happens on the training playground called "Earth" has to do with the interaction of dualities. **Whether you want it or not, you will attract a part of yourself that is subconscious to you in order to learn it better.** I talk to those of you who have already started to understand what awareness is. **If you do not understand what kind of an interaction it is, you will get into a fight.**

But your conditioned mind will explain it differently. A man who is getting married is attracting a part of himself of which he is not conscious, thinking he will experience the greatest love of his life with this part. No, he will be at war with this part until he become aware that this is his own part. Marriage licenses that are signed at the city halls are legal documents that declare the start of new wars. These wars will occur in different forms on the three lowest chakras of a human being.

Everyone has his own advantage carrying war actions on one of those levels. Someone may simply beat you up physically. Another will crush you emotionally. The third one will oppress you mentally. On the lower levels of vibrations of consciousness the relationship between a man and a woman is always a war.

People use the "weapons" they know best during this war. A man, if he is intelligent, will not use physical violence, he will use logic. A woman will hurt a man emotionally. She will seed a state of guilt in a man, and as he is not aware of his emotional sphere, this seed will germinate and grow to anger and rage. A man will retaliate, bringing a woman to rage by his logic or by physically abusing her. This war will continue until you understand that you meet and will only meet your own parts—parts of yourself that you don't see and don't understand.

When you start to understand these parts, the character of your relationship will start to change. You cannot run away here, as it is impossible to run away from yourself. You will leave one wife, but you will meet another, similar woman. Such a vision will lead you to better understand your actions. Take a look at multiple dating agencies. People run out of one relationship and jump into another, thinking their lives will get better. The matchmaking business is built on this illusion. Everything here is built on illusion, and the higher the financial stake of the game, the grander the illusion.

In order to see illusion as illusion, you do not need police, army, or government. What do police do? They assist the criminal structure. Both thief and policeman represent two sides of one duality. Governments invest money into the police, but in reality they invest into criminal structures. You become what you fight. A policeman who fights a thief turns into a thief.

— *I attract a man in a woman's body. Do I need to become a man in order for a woman to manifest her feminine side?*

— You need to see what happens to you. Why do you think you need to become a man? Do you need to become a man because this is what is currently being accepted here? Do you need to become a man because it is written in your passport that you are a man? Perhaps you should ask yourself what is the reason that you have a female model of behavior.

— *Based on what I do and on my logical thinking, I thought my behavior was masculine.*

— One does not negate another. Masculine and feminine parts are present in a human being, but the degree of their manifestation and expressivity are different. **Perhaps, you should ask yourself, "Why do I attract women who manifest themselves as men?"** Perhaps you do it in order to figure out your masculine aspect. Having the illusory notion that you attract a woman to live happily in order that she can be sweet and gentle with you, you cannot understand what happens to you. You receive what you do not expect.

When you start to investigate why this happens, your understanding of yourself and the world will be more real. When you see a part of yourself, completely unknown to you internally, sitting next to you externally, you start to investigate it. A man meets a woman to investigate the aspects of himself of which he is unaware. That's why the only thing worth doing here for the one who intends to wake up is to self-investigate. Self-investigation leads to an increase in vibrations of consciousness of a self-investigator. Everything provides an opportunity for this. When you start to look at yourself and others from this point of view, we will have a different conversation.

— *Is self-investigation the answer to the question "how"?*

— *Are we to conduct self-investigation to solve a problem?*

— What problem? Who created this problem?

— *I did.*

— And you are solving it.

— *Naturally.*

— The one who created the problem is not interested in solving it. He is interested in its maintenance. What people call a solution of the problem here is its constant prolongation. You speak from the aspect of yourself that is doing exactly that right now.

— *Does self-investigation presuppose an action of a heart sphere?*

— Yes. It also presupposes intellectual, feeling, and physical actions. You cannot divide them. I keep telling you that all three components of a human being should work together and be in sync.

People understand actions as physical actions, but prior to anything being manifested in physical action, it should be manifested in mental and emotional spheres. There would be no airplanes if someone did not to come up with an idea of an airplane, realized it in drawings, and then in physical reality.

We realize physically what is present in our intellectual and emotional spheres. But a thought devoid of energy of feelings will not give you an opportunity to create something physically. Many people talk about doing something, but never realize anything. A mental

199

form has to be saturated by strong emotion if it is to be implemented in physical reality. The cooperation between the intellectual and emotional sphere is necessary. Those who create anything here have a strong emotional sphere.

Certain ideas are accompanied by strong emotions. The ideas of Nazism and communism had strong emotional support. But the ideas of unity and multilevel consciousness we discuss here cannot be fed with the energies of these lower levels of vibrations that fed the ideas of conquest and manipulation.

A victim will always find an oppressor

— *A man and a woman sat in front of me on a bus yesterday. I decided to see them as my inner man and my inner woman. I paid very close attention to them, even though there were many other people around. What I observed was striking. They were both older than me. Both were unpleasant. The man was drunk, while the woman appeared to be of low sexual standards. The man was loudly asking her for her phone number. Initially, she refused, but finally she wrote it on a piece of paper and gave it to him. I felt that the man, despite his drunkenness, was playing a game. He clearly saw his victim and was playing a game that would help him achieve his goal. It was a calculated, cold approach that he outwardly presented as drunkenness. The woman was waving him off, but as soon as she gave him her phone number, he lost interest in her. But now, she started to talk to him: "Why are you so drunk? Try to sit up." As soon as he completed his part and lost interest, she showed herself in the role of an oppressor. She appeared to be very emotional, while he was quite calculating. That was my feeling. A woman is craving for an open heart, while a man is as yet undecided. A question was born in me: "What happens when an inner man and woman have one aim?"*

— They always have the same aim, but at the lower vibrations of consciousness it is always war. You described a man throwing a lasso at a woman. She was caught by it, and now she retaliates, pulling him back. At this level of interaction, a man has an aim of seduction, while the woman's aim is to retain him. They are co-tuned. They will never enter any game without being co-tuned. They do not understand it, but both of them are looking for actors who will play in their show, and they find them on the level of vibrations where they are. This drunkard had chosen her out of many women there. This is not a coincidence. There are no coincidences here.

Take a look at serial killers. I saw a movie about one recently. A man is depicted as killing older women. Everybody is angry and upset. Nobody understands his behavior. When he is caught, he explains, "I walk. I see a woman. I feel that I have to kill her." This is the resonance of two energies. An oppressor meets a victim, recognizes her, and performs an act of oppression. Nothing is coincidental. Things may appear coincidental, but it is just an appearance. He kills in one village and moves to the next. He walks, searches, and he kills.

— *What is the mechanism of transformation?*

— I constantly talk about it. Unless you start seeing things as they are, transformation will continue to be no more than a word for you. To see things as they are is not simple, as we can see. I think I am great and I am proud of it, but suddenly people start telling me that this is only my view of myself. The most difficult thing is to see things as they are. I speak about it without any condemnation, but the one who is told about the discrepancy between his image of himself and his real image starts to immediately experience guilt and condemnation. That makes these areas very difficult to access. You came here to evolve spiritually, but we start digging the areas you do not want to dig. "What do I need this for? This is not a spiritual evolution" — some say. But that is precisely what spiritual evolution is. It is seeing things the way they are.

When I see something in myself, it changes. It changes because I see it. But in order to see, you need to do a lot of work. You need to start doing what you are not in the habit of doing. You need to dramatize duality in order to see it. Currently, you do not see it, and therefore you cannot discern it. Through the action that is not habitual for you, you can dramatize it. It will become active. This is very uncomfortable, but this will allow you to feel and to see both sides of it. Later on, you will be able to make certain conclusions about this duality.

Without a good understanding of duality, practice, and the ability to enter it in a state of awareness, you are bound to wander in illusion. Self-investigation requires passion and courage. It requires something extraordinary. **Self-investigation will not allow you to remain asleep, i.e. to be in one side of yourself and to fight another side of yourself, expressed externally.** That is what the majority of people do.

Here we start to see the opposite sides of duality as polarities of one quality. It is very unusual. I keep telling you how it will happen and what kind of roadblocks you will encounter, so you can start feeling it and doing it on your own. I don't know whether you will do it or not. It depends on you.

You can't comprehend what self-investigation is by using the mind alone. You can enter a process and start moving in it. I describe how it happens. Certain things will occur later, but first, you need to feel the general direction of the movement toward yourself. The most difficult part is to start to move a train that stands still. When it starts to roll, it will move faster and faster. Serious effort has to be applied to move it from a stationary position. The force of inertia of the mechanical perception is very strong. What we are dealing with is the inertia of your sleeping consciousness that interferes and prevents you from starting this movement.

What happened after my leaving the seminar...

— *Can I say something? I returned to the seminar with a feeling of gratitude. As soon as I left you, I got into a difficult situation, and I think I was able to get out of this situation thanks to your teaching.*

— Great. This is after your asking for your money back and wanting to leave forever.

— *I wanted to thank you back then, but somehow I did not. I left the seminar and returned home. I found that my daughter did not return from her trip to Turkey where she was on vacation with friends. She was supposed to be home by nine p.m.. I called her friend's parents who told me that the flight was delayed and they may not arrive until morning. I could not sleep; something was bothering me. Morning comes, and still there is no news. I called the airport and found out that the flight the kids were supposed to arrive on did not exist. I called the travel agency that booked their trip. It turned out the travel agency worked through another travel agency. The money was transferred, but the sender failed to send the money to the second agency. Parents got together and went to the travel agency. We spent twenty four hours there. We were told not to get nervous and to go home, but we refused, saying we would not move until our kids were safely on board. Then we stormed the main office of the agency. We expressed our mistrust and demanded an explanation of what was being done step by step. There were two people in the office. There was a*

Russian woman there and a man who appeared to be Turkish. It turned out that the director of the travel agency escaped to Turkey with a large sum of money, and those two were not sure what to do. I started screaming at them expressing my frustration that nothing was being done. The woman said they were working on the situation and asked us to wait for another hour. We went outside again and continued to wait nervously. An hour later, I looked inside the office and saw that the "Turk" was getting ready to leave. He was the only man amongst them who appeared to be respectable. One of the parents tried to prevent him from leaving, but I explained that he was probably our only chance. He was going somewhere to address our problem, and I decided to accompany him. We got into a taxi where he told me that he had absolutely no relation to this organization and came to get his money back. To make a long story short, it was a criminal structure that was making money off the tourists, and the question was about a payment that was not made.

— You got yourself in the same situation that was played by you here. You were telling me that I was a false teacher, and you got yourself a false flight. But at the time you were not ready to understand those things.

— *The mafia also refused to pay. Parents started to go home one by one, and I understood that our kids were going to be left there all by themselves.*

— You are discussing the technical side of this situation. The psychological side is connected to what I just said. Do you understand that?

— *Yes. I am trying to make a logical connection here.*

— I am going to show you what you have inside. You did not want to hear that then. You were calling me a false-teacher, and you wanted to get your money back. This is in you. Now you are describing the situation that was created by you based on this perception. You got into the same situation of which you were accusing me.

— *I agree.*

— Those are the most important things. They need to be seen. Just to worry as a mother worries about her children is great, but unless you understand the situation, you will continue to encounter similar scenarios constantly. I am pretty sure you do.

— *But everything ended as you said it would. Now I am back here. When everyone refused to pay and left, I understood there is not going to be any plane. The "Turk" turned out to be from Baku. He was representing the Azerbaijan mafia. We were going back in a taxi talking, and I, losing my last hope, thought, "Dear God, I have the intention to save those kids. I have a very strong intention to help them." I started to dig inside, bringing up to the surface all kinds of dirty stuff. I was thinking, "Dear Lord. Please, punish me, but help those kids who got into this situation and who are not guilty at all."*

— The kids did not get into this situation by being "not guilty at all."

— *I was talking to the "Turk," and suddenly I found him to be noble. He was half Muslim and half Jew. He was practicing both beliefs. I sat there thinking that I was Christian and Buddhist who was practicing neither religion, and who now was in such a mess. I started to understand that I respected him more than I respected myself. He was supposed to be lower than me, being part of the mafia, while I was supposed to be noble. But, as it turned out, he was on a much higher level.*

— How did your story end?

— *We spent a long time talking. I almost forgot about the situation. I almost let it go, when suddenly he went to a phone, made a few phone calls, and returned saying, "A plane is leaving in thirty minutes to bring your kids back."*

— That was a long story. What exactly did you understand in this situation?

— *I understood the oppositions. What I saw in him is also in me.*

205

— The most important thing I repeat again and again: "The world and people in it are the way you see them. If you see him as mafia guy who wants to get your money, that's what you will get. If you see another side of him, and you saw that other side, you would get a different thing.

— *I told him, "You are so interesting. You know so much. Where did you learn it all?"*

— Do you understand that we are not talking about him, but you? You changed your perception. You moved to the opposite side, and you received a new situation according to this new vision. So, who changed your perception, and what would have happened were you not to change your perception? When you were here few days ago, you had a different perception. You held it very tightly. You did not want to change it. You felt insulted and resentful. You wanted to get your money back and to leave the seminar.

— *Every parent there screamed that everything was paid in full.*

— The same situation. You are constantly discussing the external manifestations of your situation, while I constantly push you to see what occurs inside of you.

— *I am not used to this yet. I am listening to you, and I try to apply it to my life.*

— So, the major point of our discussion is that the world is the way you conceive it. It is neither bad nor good; it is the way you see it. If you see it as horrific, it will be horrific. But it is you who are horrific. When you see it differently, it will be different.

— *Save yourself, and those who are close to you will be saved too.*

— What does it mean "save yourself"? Who do you need to save yourself from?

— *I am trying to say that I changed my attitude.*

206

— I understand. I am showing you the relativity of slogans. I understand what you mean. I just have to be very precise. This is my task. I cannot be content with generic statements. Some are content with them, but not me. It is not going to fly here. Every time you say something, I am going to ask you to clarify what you mean.

We are moving fast here. Perhaps you will re-experience similar situations for a couple more years. I tell you, "This is the situation. Let's become aware of it." Otherwise, we will be dragging our feet. I might not be here a few years down the road, when you would be ready to talk and come to the conclusion that I was right. You will come, but this place would be empty. That is why I am pushing you to see the basics that need to be extracted out of this situation.

— *But my pride... I become aware of the situation... I proved that the mechanism works... I was very grateful. I wanted to thank you, but I had a feeling that I was expelled.*

— If you feel expelled, you would sit here as a student who was expelled.

— *I decided not to come here while study group was in session but to arrive after it was over. But I forgot when it was supposed to be over and arrived earlier and found you here. I feel great and free now.*

— Excellent. It means that your True "I" pushes you to see more than you have seen previously. This process occurs through seeing what is the way it is. Can you describe the scenario you played in the beginning of our seminar? It will be a good marker on the road of your spiritual movement.

— *I cannot understand how I could have said what I have said. I tend to relate to teachers with such veneration.*

— That is precisely why you were able to say it.

— When I become aware of what I said and to whom I said it, I could not even comprehend where all of it came from. But this situation helped me to sort out some things in me.

From glorification to crucifixion

— You showed us another side of glorification. You entered on a wave of veneration, but then you moved to the opposite state very fast.

— I did not understand anything.

— I understand that you did not understand. The mechanical, sleeping man does not understand anything. Something just happens to him. "Jesus is coming! The Savior is coming!" A few days later, they crucify him, screaming, "You idiot! You cannot even save yourself." The same people that worshipped him now crucify him.

— I was so eager to be here.

— I understand. You were equally eager to venerate and crucify the teacher. I understand this duality very well, and I don't need your veneration that would later turn to crucifixion. That's why I stimulate the opposite to the veneration side. I invite you to come forward and to express what irritates you in me and why you hate me.

— Where did I get it?

— What do you mean, where? Please understand that your perception is dual. Everything is dual here. Your venerable part is in direct opposition to your crucifying part.

— I was reading your book Butterfly, *when suddenly I experienced a strong vibration in my solar plexus. It was very pleasant, and I thought it was connected to you.*

— Of course.

— That is how it was expressed. I liked it immediately. I was reading slowly, letting it pass through me. A few days later, a butterfly flew into my window. It was deep yellow in color. I thought it was such a good symbol. It was a beautiful butterfly. I also felt it was of the male sex. It was of such bright colors.

— You describe external things all the time. We are living in a symbolic reality. Everything here is symbolic. This reality enchants-disenchants you so much that you cannot talk about anything else. A butterfly flew in and it was beautiful. But it is only a symbol.

— Where do these feelings come from?

— I share your feeling of enchantment. However, I also say that it will change to disenchantment, and you will come here surprised. "Where did it come from?"

— I came enchanted, and I became disenchanted.

— Of course. The best way to become disenchanted is to get powerfully enchanted first. You get enchanted to the fullest. Then you meet the one who got you enchanted, and you say, "Who is this? Did I get enchanted with him?" The title of my next book is going to be *Disenchanted Enchantment*.

— My daughter says, "You read a book about a butterfly, and a butterfly flies into your window. Isn't it funny?"

— Great. Take a look at the level of materialization here. And what will happen when you read a book about the devil? You will look outside and see the devil knocking on your window asking to be let in. I keep telling you that the human being is a creator, but a creator that is not aware of what and how he creates. The creation occurs through our thoughts. When your thoughts are strongly filled with the energy of feelings, you materialize them fast. As a result, your life is in total disarray. You can materialize God knows what this way.

— Some time ago, I read Castaneda's book about human-crows. I was rushing to work one day and saw a woman dressed in black on the street. She was beautiful and well dressed. I had a sensation that she wanted to let me pass her by. She moved a little bit aside and she looked very much like a crow. I was late to work and had to rush, but I noticed it passing her by. She was walking behind me spitting and saying something under her breath.

— You need to understand something very important. When you fill your hallucinations with strong feelings, you materialize all this gibberish that is present in your conditioned mind. You need to sort out what the aware creativity is. This is the essence of our process. You react emotionally to everything. This emotionality prevails in you, but you are unable to say what you want to say. I constantly ask you this question, but you can't answer.

— I can only describe it.

— You describe precisely out of the states through which you live. And you live through them vividly, and as a result, can describe them for a very long time.

— Yes.

— You need to understand what I explain mentally. Please understand it as knowledge that is needed for self-investigation. On top of it, you missed a lot during this seminar. You need to listen attentively and to use all your intellect to understand what I say.

— I feel grateful to Nataly for coming.

— I felt very bad. I did not eat or drink. I felt I was here all the time.

— You need to be aware of these highly emotional states. Try to speak in short sentences, and to clearly express your thoughts. You may not be in the habit of doing so, but this is precisely what we do here. We do what we are not in the habit of doing. Your habit is to describe your states, the states you are not even aware of, using long periods of time. Until you understand that this is what you do, you will do it mechanically. Self-awareness will prevent you from doing it. Then the next step will come.

You should attempt to become aware of your every desire to speak now. You need to become aware that you try to speak again and again, holding yourself in the middle of a sentence. This will be the first step. If you don't do it now, you will continue to remain in the same mechanical part.

— *I am aware of three thoughts now. Where will another one come from?*

— Okay. If you are aware of the three thoughts, the appearance of the fourth thought will be great news to you.

— *True.*

— Excellent. Become aware and welcome the appearance of the new thoughts. This is what I do. I stimulate the appearance of new thoughts.

— *Nataly described a situation that mirrors this very well. This is the law of the boomerang. We change ourselves. By using these changes we can create energetic thought forms. For example, when I have negative thoughts about someone, these thoughts return to me. But what happens to another human being? Do I influence him?*

To each his own, and he will get it

— Can you not be uninfluenced in this reality? It is impossible. **Everything is interconnected here. Everyone here is looking for an actor who will help him to produce a good show. An oppressor is looking for a victim, and he will find one. A victim is looking for an oppressor, and he will find one. The one that wants to be hit will be hit. The**

211

one who wants to hit, will hit. Nothing that happens here happens for "no reason." Do you think that by starting to think negatively, you will harm an innocent human being? It's a primitive notion. No one here will receive anything for no reason, and no one will transmit anything for no reason. It is impossible. You cannot hurt someone unless this someone wants to be hurt.

You start to think negatively about someone, and you think that something bad is going to happen to him. But if you don't think negatively about him, other people will. He will attract them. This is the law of resonance. You attract the vibrations you are currently in. If you are in the negative vibrations, you attract the situations of the negative vibrations.

As the majority of people happen to be in the lower vibrations, they attract nothing but these vibrations. The "victim—oppressor" game is the basic game that is played in the lowest frequencies of consciousness, i.e. in the old matrix of conscience. Therefore, what is considered to be goodness here is just another side of evil, but the conditioned mind cannot understand the interrelationship between the opposite sides of duality, and as a result, it always acts in the dark.

The main question is not who and how I can hurt, but what do I do in order to get to the next, higher level of vibration of consciousness? To simplify, a human being brings as much harm as he brings benefit. You can call harm benefit or benefit harm—it is the same thing. How do you know what is benefit and what is harm?

During our earlier conversation, you behaved "weirdly." You said that my behavior was inappropriate, and you run away from the seminar. You thought that I caused you harm. You accused me of being a false teacher, but later it turned out I caused something that was beneficial to you. Did you understand that this was goodness earlier? No. Another example is the exercise we did earlier, hitting each other while being aware of what the one who is being hit was feeling. Hitting people on the cheek is not considered to be a good thing to do here, but the result of this exercise provided you with opportunities to become aware, which is goodness. It turns out that the notions of the conditioned mind regarding what is good and what is evil are illusory.

— *Can I add something to the topic of good and evil? Yesterday you mirrored my notion of what a man is. You mirrored my state. You showed me how my man suppresses feelings. I saw myself being afraid of a man, thinking he can humiliate me. That is why I should not feel. I am grateful for what you have done.*

— Wait.

— *I have not finished yet. I am going to finish when I want to finish.*

— No. Let's finish when I want to finish. Look how excited you are. On one side you thank me, but on the other side you don't let me say a word.

— **Yes, I am excited. You constantly interrupt me.**

— **Yes, I interrupt you, and I do it with a certain aim. No one can make resentful someone who is not resentful. However, the one who is ready to be resentful will always find a reason to be resentful. He will also always find the one who will make him resentful. The one who wants to be insulted is impossible not to insult, he will always find those who will insult him.**

— *That's what you have showed me yesterday. I was perplexed.*

— You are trying to show how amazingly aware you are. You got excited. You keep talking and talking. "Shut up! Do not interrupt me! Let me express my very spiritual thoughts!" You don't like it? Tomorrow you will come again, saying, "He

213

mirrored me so well yesterday. I experienced a spiritual rebirth." This is a fairy tale about a white horse.

— *I come here to tell fairy tales.*

— *You said the same thing yesterday.*

— We are tired of this. We heard about the white horse; tell us about the dark one.

— *I want to talk about the white horse, and I will talk about the white for now.*

— We are all tired of you.

— *Yesterday, when everyone laughed, I saw that everyone was judging me.*

— Oh, how proud I am! Everyone is judging me, but I will talk about the white horse! You create these situations when people judge and hate you, and you are experiencing kaif from these situations. You don't want to part with this scenario. You talk about the white horse all the time, while I talk about the black one, the one you are so afraid of.

— *I saw this black horse yesterday.*

— Two friends were passing an oral exam in biology. Both learned a great deal about fleas and could answer any question pertaining to fleas. One of them picked a ticket with a question that dealt with fleas. He told the teacher everything about fleas. Another was picking ticket after ticket without luck. Questions about other insects would come up. Finally, he said, "My ticket is about a dog whose fur is infested with fleas." And he started talking about fleas.

— *What do you mean?*

— Everyone here is waiting to jump in with his line that others know by heart by now and are tired of. Are you mechanical or not?

— *How do you tolerate us?*

— *Pint has his own song to sing.*

214

— *He experiences the Truth, while we are singing our songs.*

— My function is to bring your habitual program to malfunction. For the program, it is deadly. If you do not speak up your program, you will not be satisfied. If you are fast enough and able to insert a few mechanical words from your program, you will praise the seminar. You will say it was great. I got up on a chair, everyone looked at me, and I was singing my song for five minutes. Twenty people listened to me.

— *I outdid myself. My speech was longer than last time.*

— Yes, and we are all interested in more people being here. In this case, more people will hear our song. And my function is to collect a crowd for your feature presentation. People are coming to my seminar, and you can sing your song here. Now I understand why you come here and pay money for the seminar. You want to sing your song, and you want people to hear you. Well, the price to sing these songs will go up now.

Okay. Now I am going to turn the music on and ask you to feel what is going on inside of you.

— *Over the last few days women were talking a lot about "father." It started to bother me. I saw my father only one time. I was fifteen then. I have never pronounced the word "father." My older brother was three when I was born, and a few weeks later my mother left my father. She told me that one day he had thrown me, wrapped in blankets, into a corner of a room. I was thinking about it yesterday, and I felt I was in the room where it happened. It turns out he did not throw me, he was choking me. He was having sex with my mother when I woke up crying. He got up and tried to choke me. I am asking him now, "Why dad? Why are you doing this?" He screams, "I hate you." I tell him, "I love you. I love you. I love you." I repeat it many times. My right hand starts to burn. Afterwards, he picks me up and tries to console me. Then I saw myself at six years old. I had a younger brother, Peter. Mom went outside and asked me to look after him. I just recalled a scene of me choking him. When mother got back, I was sitting on top of him and choking him. When I felt paternal love toward a child, I started telling Peter I loved him and started to baby him instead of choking him. I also felt love toward my older brother who was killed. I saw all the men that were important in my life, and I felt love and gratitude toward them. At that time Evgenia touched my left leg and started to caress it. I was observing it, and I did not want to withdraw it as I habitually do. Then my right arm got tingly. At that time, I said goodbye to father. That was the first time in my life that I pronounced the word "father."*

— I saw moving colors. They were violet-black, predominantly black. I felt separation. I felt my head separate from my body. My head was coming up with orders, while my body was in a state of bliss. Usually, I am a cold woman who forbids herself a lot. I frequently experiment with myself. I can never relax fully. I am unable to see. I feel, but don't see anything.

— I sensed the dissonance between the upper and the lower part of my body. When the upper part starts to vibrate, the lower part turns into an anchor and vice versa. These parts were unable to interact. Then I started to keep an eye on the pictures. I started to feel some painful moments in interaction between a man and a woman. This duality was activated strongly during this seminar. I told myself yesterday that I would spread up the duality "man—woman," because I do not understand where my man is and where my woman is. Certain events started to occur. I observe them now.

— A man comes to a doctor, pulls out his dick and says, "Cut it." The doctor asks, "Why cut such a great thing?" The man says, "Cut it. There is not enough blood for two of us. When he is up, I have to lie down."

216

CHAPTER 5

GUILT IS THE OPPOSITE SIDE OF CONDEMNATION

◆━◆・◆━◆・◆━◆・◆━◆・◆━◆・◆━◆・◆━◆・◆━◆・◆━◆・◆━◆・◆━◆・◆━◆・

The chorus of dead people sings song to life

— *Yesterday during midafternoon tea, I heard many definitions. The words "awareness" and "enlightenment" were heard in many different combinations and broken down to parts. Wars. I saw the games my mind plays trying to measure, weigh, and define everything, measure and weigh it in order to put everything in certain brackets. To speak in order to speak. Nonstop. To get pleasure out of speaking certain smart words. I also observed myself being scared while listening to five people speaking simultaneously. When I listened to this chorus, I wanted to scream, "Enough!" I went outside into the snow. Everything cleared up for me outside. I wanted to thank you for this chorus. I saw myself from the side in this group of voices. I saw many competing parts of me, juggling and trying to define things, when in reality the topic discussed was quite simple and only required these parts to be silent for a minute.*

— A chorus of dead people singing song to life the way they imagine it to be.

— *For the first time in my life, I experienced something without expectations. These seven days were so filled for me that I will relive and re-experience them for a long time, assimilating what happened. I noticed that I behaved as natural as I could here. I noted my theatricality based on previous conversations and actions, and at the same time I was constantly ready to reply to anything, to tune into something. There was this lightness. It is a new state.*

— Out of awareness of the state you are in right now, something new can come. But in order to become aware of this state, a deep inner work needs be done. The conditioned mind is an obstruction to this work. Look, I repeat the same thing in different ways all the time. If this was an intellectual activity, you would have gotten it at the end. If not the first time, you would have gotten it the second or third time around. I use simple words, but still you do not understand.

It means you cannot understand it based on intellect alone. **Understanding presupposes new knowledge and living through it, experiencing it.** In order to do that, it is necessary for your feeling sphere to start working, accepting the opposite. In order to accept the opposite that happens to be in your subconsciousness, you need to see it. And to see it is frightening for the one who is in the old matrix of consciousness.

— *When I don't attract something on purpose, when everything happens naturally, much more happens that is lived through, felt, and remembered—something is simply unfolding.*

— The Impulse of the Soul cannot be expressed in words. One cannot know how it will be realized, but one can follow it. When one follows this Impulse, something very important starts to occur. Otherwise, you try to plan everything using

218

your conditioned mind, repeating the same thing over and over again.

What happens during our process? What do we do here? We integrate the fragmented consciousness, i.e. the structure that is called personality, and that is considered to be the only real thing here. But personality is just a projection that has its own apparatus of thoughts and notions that do not allow it to get in touch with what gave it life, with the Soul and the Spirit.

Our process provides an opportunity to find who you truly are. In order to do this, you have to have passion. Without passion, it is useless. That is why a selection process is important. We don't need many people. If you have the Impulse of the Soul, the atmosphere is created that will provide an opportunity for self-remembrance. When people gather together arguing who is smarter, better, or more enlightened, it leads to the lowering of vibrations and makes our work impossible.

— *I want to thank everyone here. During last two days I felt liberated. I felt liberated on a mental, emotional, and physical level. The sore throat, constant congestion, headaches, and multiple other symptoms that I considered to be negative and unpleasant, I now see as liberating the physical body.*

— Correct. This is a result of your cells being saturated with the energy of higher quality. They move to another regimen of work. Energies of lower quality manifest themselves in what is called a disease here. **Any disease is simply a resistance.** When I understand what is happening, I have a different relationship with it.

— *Interestingly, only my right side is hurting. The left side is taking it calmly.*

— We are not living right now but are reviewing yesterday's films and getting excited. I am tired of "was, yesterday I felt good, I felt this, and I felt that…" What about now?

— In true reality, there is no past and no future; everything is simultaneous. But here we have all of this. We have to be in two worlds: in this world, but not of this world. When you are in both worlds at once, you will be able to use the terminology of this illusory world, while understanding its illusory nature. You will say, "There is past and there is future," while understanding that in reality there is only Present. The majority of people only have the past, and they build their future on it. That is where their nostalgia is coming from. The exit to the state of timelessness in the beginning is very unusual. It is frightening for the personality. But later on, fortified in this new perception of time, you understand that linear time is an illusion.

— By not expressing one's feelings and emotions, one is neither fish nor meat.

— What are you trying to say?

— What is he then?

— I constantly ask you to think before you speak. You say something without thinking all the time.

— I remember an old joke: "Good will conquer evil, bring it to its knees, and put a bullet in its head."

— I saw that the state one is in is of utmost importance. When I am in my habitual, usual state of consciousness, I have the same thoughts all the time. In that state, irritation and other negative emotions appear. It seems that I am about to figure out what exactly it is that irritates me, but in reality, no work is done. Repetition of the same thing occurs. When one is in another state of consciousness, those thoughts are absent, there is no irritation. And it is not necessary to talk about things one wanted to talk about while being in that state of consciousness. One cannot

220

understand what to work with in such a state, because one does not want to work in it. And in another state there is something to work with, but no work is being done.

To be in two worlds simultaneously

— There are two banks of one river. We need to have a bridge. Without a bridge, there would not be any changes. I can suddenly show up on one bank without problems and irritation. Everything is great there. But what did I do on this bank? Suddenly, I am back on the old bank, and the new bank is a fuzzy memory. Now I don't understand how I got there and what I did there.

— *One is afraid to whisper a word in that state out of fear of flipping back.*

— Look, to be in two worlds simultaneously is of utmost importance to us. In order to do that you need to master this world. You need to become fully aware of what the conditioned mind creates here. You cannot bypass the work with dualities. Thanks to that work, you will be able to switch your mind to different mode, to different vibrations. As for now, it is still in the old matrix. Eastern esoteric schools recommend, "Don't think."

What does it mean, "Don't think?" Can you cross a street without thinking? Do you need to sit at home meditating for twenty years? Are you to become a saint? People come to him, wash him, dress him, feed him, and put him back on his chair. He is just sitting there. He is not in this world already, but they wash and feed his body that happens to be in this world. You don't need to be a mummy. You will not be able not to think because the mind is a creative apparatus. To not think means to not create. Then die. Why are you sitting here? If you live here, you create. But what do you create? You can create in separation, being unaware of dualities, or clearly seeing them. When you see a full spectrum of duality, you can play it as you play a piano.

When you don't see duality, you behave as a drunken pianist who, dozing off, presses one of the outermost keys of the instrument repeatedly. A piano has many keys, but your pianist only presses one. The pianist on the opposite side presses the opposite key. These two argue all the time about whose music is better. That is what they are preoccupied with. When duality is mastered, one can play all the keys, creating a beautiful music.

— *When I see a duality I activate, I condemn the opposite side. I see what I am about to say now. It will be coming from my habitual side. I am aware of it.*

— You have an illusion that you see it. You are just using words. This is gibberish. For me to see and to be aware is the same thing. I can see only when I am aware. **The more aware I am of something, the more I see.** You are just using those words. How can you see if you are not aware? And if you are aware, tell us everything in detail. That is what I am waiting for.

— *I will try to describe the mechanism. I am sitting here, and I see my usual duality, my program manifesting itself. I see that I am speaking now not to become aware, but to satisfy my program again.*

— **If you see it, talk about it. Otherwise, you don't see it.**

— Then I don't see it.

— Then stop using the words "see" and "aware." You are not using them correctly. If I see it, I can clearly describe it. And if I create an illusion, I would say that I see, but for some reason I do not understand exactly what I see. That is the

222

method by which a sleeper brings everything to sleep. He hears a new word, repeats it, and falls asleep again, dreaming a dream in which he develops spiritually.

— *So, it means I simply feel something. I feel irritated by something.*

—**We need to be specific. What irritates you? Be specific. That's what I am waiting for. You can say, "Yesterday I felt irritated by Peter. I met Peter and we started talking about it. We figured out which dualities provoked our irritation, and now I am going to describe them." That's awareness.**

— *To be specific, yesterday I was telling everyone here how each one of them irritated me. I saw the duality "smart—stupid" in everyone. You told me I repeat myself. I recalled my thoughts. I am trying to sort them out, not to repeat myself again.*

— You are constantly analyzing. I already explained to you what you are doing. You approach your lover saying, "Dear, let me analyze you." You do it all the time.

— *Yes. I have a strong desire to judge everyone.*

—**Analysis leads to condemnation. We explicitly reviewed how judgment converts to condemnation. Analysis is judgment. For example, I judge that I am taller than Maria. This is just a judgment. Based on the height of my body, I am taller. But when I say that I am better than Maria because I am taller, I start to condemn. That's how judgment converts to condemnation. The mind constantly gives birth to different judgments. You cannot change this. You cannot stop the work of the mind.** Otherwise, you would not be able to discern anything. You would get up in the morning and have no idea where you are. You would not know where your legs are. You would not know where your arms are. You would not know floor from ceiling. What would you do then? You would pee in bed.

Judgments are necessary. The mind operates based on judgment, but the ego converts judgment to condemnation. That's what personal or personality pride is based upon.

— I closed my eyes, and I asked why I destroy men. I saw a cold snake that needs to be warmed up. This is the way she receives energy, calling it love.

— What should I do if I want to be warm? I don't kill in order to get this warmth. If I kill someone, there would not be any warmth in him. There would be a cold, dead body, and I would receive this cold. In desiring warmth, you need to give out warmth. If you want to be rich—give your riches to others. If you want to be smart—give your thoughts to others. If you want to be aware—create opportunities for others to become aware. The more you give, the more you receive. But the old matrix of consciousness puts it differently: if I don't have it, I have to receive it any way I can. Then I start to manipulate others, not seeing that others are me.

— Yesterday I observed the mechanism of duality "condemnation—guilt." It is probably the most mechanical duality as it is very difficult to see. I frequently say and hear from others that as soon as one sees something, one immediately starts saying that one is sitting in garbage. So, factually, I negate myself.

From condemnation to judgment

— I keep telling you there is no garbage. There is no shit. As soon as you say the word "garbage" or "shit," you condemn. You do not utilize judgment; you immediately transfer to condemnation. When you condemn something, you experience guilt that is built on the same grounds. We need to see the judgment behind condemnation, and we need to understand that judgment can be different. We don't need to condemn the judgments of others. **THE TRANSITION FROM CONDEMNATION TO JUDGEMENT IS A PROCESS OF AWARENESS**. But, as you can see now, this is not an easy process. It is much easier to condemn using meaningless, insulting words.

This is a typical approach toward others that people use. People point their fingers at others: "You are sitting in shit, and he is sitting in shit. Everyone is sitting in big pile of shit, but not me." What kind of judgment is this? It is pure condemnation. In order to start making judgments, one has to develop the mind. But people do not want to develop the mind. It is much easier to scratch one's pride using the most primitive method of calling others names. You need to move from condemnation to judgment, i.e. you need to start to identify dualities and to review them in detail. This is the necessary work of the mind we have to do.

— *That's what I saw early in the morning after the holotrop. I noticed that I was very irritated for no apparent reason. It took me a while to see that I jumped out of my habitual role, which for the mind is always anxiety provoking—it starts to be busy right away.*

— Yes, those are not comfortable states. I want to repeat. This is not easy. It is comfortable to condemn if you are in the habit of doing it. And everyone is in the habit of doing it. We do it constantly. It is very uncomfortable to transfer to a state of judgment. I would invite you to tell us what irritates you. Perhaps, someone will become *aware* during the seminar on awareness. Start with specifics. What irritates you?

— *I did not want to share a room with Larisa. I took it with offense.*

— Why?

225

— *I am irritated by her intellectual show. She suppresses me. Do this. Don't do that. You show too much emotion. You talk too much.*

— And what do you do?

— *That is what I do.*

— Excellent. We don't like others to show us what we are. We are going to get irritated, and we are going to condemn those that show us who we really are.

— *Yesterday I even stepped outside onto the balcony. She walks in and I am not there. I thought I would listen to music to calm myself down. But I was unmanageable. I thought I would get violent with her. I could have kicked her out of the room.*

— You did not think about kicking yourself out.

— *I spoke to her, and I saw myself in her: my usual irritation, my usual unacceptance.*

— Specifics. Irritated by what? What does she condemn?

— *She condemns my emotionality. She condemns my talking a lot.*

— Your low vibrational emotionality.

— *Looks like it.*

— Looks like it or that is what it is?

— *I see it in myself. Right now I am getting irritated.*

— **What exactly irritates you now? Irritation is the indicator. It indicates you don't see something. While you are in a state of irritation, you do not see what exactly happens inside you. If I see a pointer, it does not mean I see where it is pointing. Irritation is a pointer. What does it point to?**

— *It points to my constantly being in a rush and my inability to see and to accept my being in a rush. I also don't see my constant talking being in the lower emotions. It seems to me that I talk very intelligently to people.*

— Excellent. What do you need to do now? You saw a pointer. You understand what it points you toward. It points

226

to your yammering. It points to your low vibrational emotions. Now you have to catch yourself in it. You start to yammer and oops, in the middle of a sentence you stop and become aware of your state.

— *How can I stop in the middle of it?*

— You can continue, but then the reason we gather here is not going to happen.

— *You were very irritated by Pint yesterday. You are not talking about it.*

— I irritate you because I am doing what you are supposed to be doing yourself. I stop you when you cannot stop yourself. You need to do it yourself. When you start to do it yourself, your irritation toward me will disappear and gratitude will arise, because I am doing for you what you need to do yourself, and you resist it. You need to stop talking now, and I say, "Stop talking."

— *I see a man that is choking a woman who wants to say something. That is it.*

— *I just saw how difficult it is for me to say certain true words. I am irritated by me easily talking gibberish, but what is true and needs to be said, I conceal. It irritates me.*

The Truth can't be spoken, but one can become aware of it

— Excellent. The ego is constantly in it. Condemnation will find its way out. One can condemn anything. If we evolve spiritually, we will condemn the spiritless. It is irrelevant to us what to condemn. The ego will always decide who and what to condemn.

— I catch myself thinking I can condemn anyone here. I don't do it. I am trying to understand what this means. This tendency is always present.

— Which tendency?

— The tendency to condemn. I have a strong necessity to condemn someone.

— Correct. That's the necessity of lower vibrations. They need to condemn. Everyone here is preoccupied with one thing only—condemnation. It is done automatically.

— It is very painful to dig it out of yourself.

— If this pain is transformed, it will not come back. Otherwise, it will resurface again and again. I work with what I have. If we only have condemnation and guilt here, how can I not work with it? Do you want me to work with illusions? Do you want me to avoid touching painful spots? You want me to caress everyone's head saying, "You are so spiritual. You grew three chakras from yesterday. You are amazing." Is that what you want? If that's the case, go and find a place where you will be caressed and put to sleep.

— I am being hit at every seminar. As soon as I open my mouth, I am hit.

— What do you want?

— I don't want anything. It hurts a lot.

— Become aware of this pain. This is a result of your inner separation. Until you see this separation, there will be nothing to connect. My role is to show it to you.

— I do that twenty four hours a day.

— You argue now. You project your not understanding and resistance onto me. You condemn me as if I am the one who caused it in you.

— I condemn myself for my coming to this world in a female body.

— Yes, but look around you. Everyone is in the same shoes. Millions of people are in the same shoes here. Are we going to commit a mass suicide? Actually, that is what civilization is moving toward. The Third World War will come and no one will be left behind because many have this attitude: "Screw everything." One should not destroy oneself but get reborn in a different state. I repeat again, a human being is a multilevel system. At the next level of consciousness, all of this is perceived as an illusion. You see this as an illusion and you are grateful to this illusion.

— *Can one transform this feeling of pain, and seeing it, laugh at oneself?*

— Laugh.

— *Perhaps one has to live through it, and then it will dissolve.*

— *You know, Natasha, during my first seminar I felt very much like Olga does now. I was suffering and felt a lot of pain. Pint asked me, "Can you laugh about your pain? Can you laugh at what was painful for you?" I started to cry even more, saying, "How can one laugh at something that hurts so much?" And before today's seminar, I spoke to someone about it, and I laughed. I spoke about myself and not about myself at the same time. I laughed about it. I saw the tragedy I lived through from a side. I saw how I created it, and I laughed about it.*

— *One has to step aside a bit in order to see something.*

— By itself, laughter does not mean anything. Russian comedian Zadornov condemns Americans and makes everyone laugh. Laughter has different manifestations. You are constantly getting attached to the external markers. When you become aware of something, your left foot may start to itch, requiring you to scratch it. It does not mean this will happen to everyone. You can start recommending that people scratch their feet, and to use this technique to become enlightened. The major thing is not in the external visible, but in the

229

invisible that is behind the visible. It is irrelevant whether you cough, laugh, sneeze, or scratch yourself during it. It is important to become aware.

You are playing a show. When you understand that you are just an actor in this show, it stops being a burden. Until you feel it to be your heavy life, it will continue to burden you. Start seeing your life as a show. This will lead to gratitude.

— *Do you bring it to a head in order for me to experience a feeling of guilt?*

Search for the invisible that hides behind the visible

— Look how difficult it is to touch these things. When you start touching fear, conversation about it is viewed as condemnation, an insult, unacceptance because it causes you to feel guilty. You say, "You make me feel guilty." I say, "No. Nobody makes you guilty. Guilt appears in you. I just show you what we have here the way it is, but you are unable to see it without condemnation and guilt. You condemn yourself for it. I don't condemn you for anything. You do it yourself."

— *I condemn others, and then I condemn myself for it.*

— You do it, not me.

— *You started this conversation, brought up this theme, and I reacted to it.*

— You just said that I brought up this conversation in order to condemn you.

— *Yes.*

— And I tell you, I don't do it to blame and condemn. I speak about things as they are, but those who are identified with their fear will say that I condemn them. I do not condemn them, but they can't understand that. It is difficult to touch those things. That's why it is so important to select people that are ready for this work.

— *I caught my thought that I also want to pity her now. The next thought is that if I were to pity her, it would only reinforce her and me in condemnation and guilt.*

— The desire to pity someone arises out of pity toward oneself because we are all in the same situation. So, keep tracing the states that arise in you. Will you condemn me, pity her, or pity yourself? These mechanical reactions are downloaded in personality. The state of guilt is extremely difficult to experience. Condemnation feels better than guilt. Therefore, I am going to condemn. I don't feel guilty, but I condemn everyone. It is easy to condemn. It is very painful and heavy to feel and to remain in the state of guilt. But those are similar things. In order to not feel this guilt, I will condemn mechanically, without even understanding it. I will condemn everyone, especially those who are pointing me toward it. That is why condemnation is so widespread here. But to feel guilt as another side of condemnation is not easy. When you condemn, you simultaneously experience guilt. **And the more you condemn, the more guilt you accumulate.**

— *I started to project condemnation onto you because I started to feel guilty.*

— Because you are afraid of guilt. So, live through this guilt as a fact: "Yes, I am guilty." Experience it. It is easy to condemn. I am strong, proud, and I am going to push everyone around. Condemnation is the active position in life. Guilt is a passive position.

— *It is very painful to be guilty.*

231

— But you are in pain. Everyone here is in pain, screams because of it, but pretends he is not, because he condemns. They think that by condemning someone, they will not feel that pain. It reminds me of a funny Jewish tale. Abraham and Sarah are in bed. Abraham is awake. He keeps turning around, preventing Sarah from falling asleep. Sarah asks him, "What's up?" Abraham replies, "I owe Isaac a thousand dollars." Sarah jumps out of bed, runs to the window and screams, "Isaac! Isaac! Wake up! Abraham owes you a thousand dollars. He is not going to pay you back." She gets back to bed, turns to Abraham, and says, "Sleep tight. Let him worry now."

It turns out guilt is much more painful to live through, because it is a passive state.

— *It is a suppressed state.*

— Okay. When I condemn, I am proud and knowledgeable. I tell the truth. When I feel guilty, I am crushed. I am nobody. And because condemnation and guilt go hand in hand, when you carry condemnation, you simultaneously carry guilt. Not wanting to experience guilt, I will enforce condemnation. As soon as I start to experience pangs of guilt, I say that it is not because of me; someone else is to be blamed. Let's condemn him.

That is how revolutions and wars start. When guilt accumulates, a scape goat must be found, condemned, and a holy war declared. People frequently talk about repentance, but it is just a way to suppress guilt. To repent is not enough. You need to understand duality. Otherwise, guilt will convert to condemnation. This is what happens all the time. To repent, when this word is used correctly, means to become aware. To repent means to understand that when you condemn someone, you simultaneously load yourself with guilt. Become aware of guilt and condemnation as two sides of one coin.

This is real repentance. But one has to walk through the phase of guilt in order to become aware of its connection to condemnation.

What happens in childhood? A child did something that is considered to be wrong. Parents immediately say, "That's it. Time out. Go to your room and feel guilty. You need to apologize." A child is forced to feel guilty. So, he develops rejection, blaming the parents.

— *During the last two days, I thoroughly felt those states. I saw how condemnation and guilt transfer from one to another. I felt that when I condemn someone, guilt is being projected. Then I feel hate, that returns later on, making me experience equal guilt associated with a heavy state of "self-punishment" for my prior condemnation.*

We feel guilty for the same thing we condemn

— We are constantly occupied with condemnation. In condemning someone, we accumulate guilt. Take a look at how much you condemn through the day. This is how much guilt you have. And how much guilt do you accumulate in one month? How much guilt do you accumulate in one year? How much guilt do you accumulate during a lifetime? We have to become aware of guilt and to experience it as the opposite side of condemnation. That will show that, in reality, truth is not what you consider it to be. **The one that condemns consider himself to be right. Otherwise, he would not condemn.**

— *During the previous seminar, we talked about seeing fortune in misfortune. If one is to see a misfortune as an experience to be observed, seen, and converted into awareness, then everything here is material for awareness. The experience of your husband was such and such, but for you it is an opportunity to see it from the side, and to become aware. It's an opportunity to see fortune in misfortune. If it was not for that situation, you would not be here, and you would have nothing to become aware of.*

— I would invite all of you to share your own guilt feelings towards someone present here.

— I feel guilty towards you. I came with certain feelings. You disappointed me, and I expressed completely opposite feelings.

— Guilt is experienced as the result of something. What did you do? What did you think? Speak the facts.

— I condemned.

— Did you condemn me?

— How could I condemned you, when I experienced completely opposite feelings?

— You are not aware of your feelings. You experienced certain feelings, and then you experienced different feelings. I told you right away that you walked in here feeling elated and euphoric, and then moved down to hell. This is natural. I know. That's how it happens. But you don't know it yet. You condemned me, and you feel guilty for this condemnation. And this guilt brought up the situation of your kids being stuck in the airport.

— I don't feel it now.

— It is important to see that any condemnation is connected to guilt. Until you understand what is hiding behind guilt, i.e. become aware of the connection between condemnation and guilt that you yourself gave birth to, nothing will happen. You created it, and you pay for it. You receive the consequences of your own actions. You do not understand the causes of these actions. We are sorting them out now. You feel guilty. Look at your

234

guilt and try to figure out what specific condemnation of yours gave birth to this guilt. When you become aware of guilt and condemnation, they will disappear.

— *What if the feeling of guilt remains?*

— Toward whom and in regards to what?

—*Coming to the seminar, I had a fight with my girl. I told her I needed to go. She did not want me to come here. I broke her resistance.*

— So, I condemned her for her inability to understand that I had to drive here. I condemned her, and I pronounced a sentence. I drove here with it, and now I experience this sentence myself because I condemned myself. It appears to me that I condemned her, but I always condemn myself, only myself.

— *That is what I wanted to ask. We are coming from the side of condemnation. I condemned her. But where is the guilt? If I experience a feeling of guilt, it means I had condemned.*

— Yes. And during that process you did not condemn someone. You condemned yourself. Whenever I blame someone, I blame myself and only myself.

— *And if we were to dig deeper? What do I condemn in myself?*

— You need to be more specific. What did you say to your girlfriend?

— *You don't understand how important it is for me. You can't get it. I have to get up and go.*

— That can be stated as a fact, but it can also be said with condemnation. There are two parts inside. One feels that there is something very important, but another says that nothing new is necessary, everything is good the way it is. So, one part of you condemns another part of you.

— *Okay. The part that says that everything is normal and does not want any changes, plays a role of my opponent, and I condemn him for his not understanding.*

235

Awareness is outside of duality. That's why it does not condemn

— Yes. And another part wants changes. But these are two sides of one coin. This is not awareness yet. **Awareness occurs when you see two sides simultaneously. When awareness of two opposite sides of duality is present, there is no conflict between them. But there is a conflict between your sides. There is a part of you that wants to evolve, and there is a part that does not want to evolve. They are two parts of one coin. Awareness sees each side as a given, the way it is.**

So, awareness is outside duality. Otherwise, you can say that you have this amazing part that wants to evolve and a bad part that does not want it to happen. And you identify with a part that wants to evolve. But the part that wants to evolve leans on the opposite part that does not want to evolve. They work together. How does the one that evolves know whether it is evolving or not? It needs to have a contrast, an opposition. Awareness observes the interaction of both parts.

— *In this particular situation, two parts which oppose each other are present. One wants something, while another does not. How is one to regulate the situation?*

— First, you need to express both of them in order to discern them, i.e. to see them together. Then you start to see that they are necessary to each other. You track down the character of their interaction. You start to understand that their relationship only appears to be conflicting. In reality, this is a necessary mutual influence that allows you to receive a certain experience you need. We already discussed this during our discussion of a duality "spiritual—material." The seeker starts to activate a duality in order to receive a certain experience.

In your case, the spiritual is your evolving part, while the material is your non-evolving part. They start to confront and wrestle each other. During this wrestling match you start to understand this duality. Awareness stands above duality and observes both sides of it. I want to repeat, you can acquire experience only by activating the interaction of the opposites. This phase is impossible to skip. Without it you will not receive an experience. That is the major difficulty.

— *What if a certain experience has been experienced to the point of nausea.*

— Then you need to stretch it to the point of **severe** nausea.

— *It is very nauseating.*

— It is not sufficiently nauseating yet.

— *My situation is related to the seminar. Those two desires, to go— not to go, pull me to pieces. I go, but my resistance is so strong that it manifests itself in external reality. I was walking my dog before coming here, and it was bitten by another dog.*

— And she said to herself, "Do not go to the seminar."

— *That's right. My dog is weak, shaky, and does not want to go outside. I am submerged in guilt, because my interest in awareness leads to the torment of my dog. The dog senses everything.*

— Your poor dog happens to represent your poor part that does not want any changes. Look, this experience is connected to crucifixion in the opposites. This is a crucifixion.

— *This is going overboard.*

— It will become more "overboard" until you fully investigate this duality. When you go to the seminar not wanting to go, when your dog is bitten all over, when your

237

clothes are torn, and when you are given a black eye—that's when you will receive the experience of this duality. How long it will take for you to accumulate this experience and to understand what exactly that duality is depends on you. **And trust me, your suffering is mediocre compare to the sufferings of other people who became aware of this duality. Some people burned for it.**

— *In my case, it transfers to a feeling of guilt.*

— Guilt is always present. We have reviewed its mechanism. I repeat, walking through duality stretches two opposite sides of it. This is very painful. I will repeat it again and again. This is how it is. This is how it should be. You cannot bypass it. You think it is easy to get above your old experience? No. I show you how duality works. The accumulation of the experience in a certain duality requires its stretching, i.e. crucifixion. You have to put yourself on a cross and nail yourself to it. The spiritual drama of Jesus Christ is a cosmic show that reveals the mechanism of liberation from the crucifixion on the cross of dualities.

— *I noticed that the resistance of the external world appears as a consequence of my inner tension. It happens, for example, when I want to go to the seminar. I want them to feel guilty for not sharing my desire to evolve, or I want to feel guilty myself for my leaving them. But when this resistance is absent, they easily let me go.*

— Exactly. Look, the understanding of duality on the lower level occurs in conflict and fight. When I go to the seminar in order to show others that they are lower than me, I produce blame and feel guilty. But I can do it differently. I can go to the seminar because I understand that I need it, while they are free to do what they want depending on their understanding or not understanding. I do not blame anyone for it, and then their blame of me resolves. Their blaming me is actually my blaming them, i.e. my blaming myself.

To end the experience of a certain duality means to end the blame and guilt connected to this particular duality. If you do not complete the process, the experience will continue to accumulate. Which one of you and for how long needs this continuation in order to see this, I do not know. If you have difficulty seeing a duality, you need to stretch it as wide as you can. This is a painful process. Your vision is weak, and you need to stretch and intensify a duality. Only when a duality is stretched to its limits will you be able to start to discern its separate sides. Otherwise, you will remain asleep.

— *My goal for this seminar has been achieved. I just saw how three dualities united in one. The first one is "spiritual—material." The second one is "condemnation—guilt." I condemned her by putting every single thing on its shelf, but it did not help her. My health was getting weaker and weaker, passive resentment was building up. The third duality deals with sexuality: our getting cold to each other. I saw the knot. I saw these three pairs with which I needed to work. It appears that all three were resolved.*

— Your vision will get broader. These problems, or the personality structure that creates these problems, will remain. You will continue to work on the same themes, but the level of your seeing them will change. What you see now is your starting point on a stretch of the road of your marathon toward yourself. At the next portion of the marathon, it will change.

— *I don't understand. Are you saying these three dualities will not disappear?*

— No. They will change. When you see the entire way that you run through on your way to yourself, you will understand why and for what reasons everything was created the way it was created in your life. Any given personality reflects the structure and working mechanisms of this reality or the old matrix of consciousness. It is built in a very special way, in order for a given personage to acquire experience. It reflects all mechanisms working in the old matrix. When you understand yourself, you will understand the world.

When you see your guilt, you can see your blame

— Who experiences guilt here?

— *I feel guilty towards men. For example, towards Oleg and Antony.*

— What kind of guilt is it, and which particular blame of yours gave birth to it?

— *Blame?*

— **Your guilt appeared as a result of your blaming Oleg and Antony. You blame them for something, not seeing that this blame gives birth and makes you feel guilty towards them. What are you blaming them for?**

— *I blame Oleg for his sexuality.*

— By blaming him, you feel guilty at the same time. Take a look at how the mechanism of blame and guilt operates. It is a snake biting its own tail. When a snake bites its own tail, its beginning and its end unite. The beginning is blame and the end is guilt. It appears that they are totally unrelated, but now we can see that they are two sides of one coin.

— *I blame Antony for his silence.*

— By blaming Antony, you blame yourself for silence, and you feel guilty about it. And what is your silence about?

— *I blame myself for not speaking up. I do have something to say.*

240

— I blame him for not speaking when he has something to say, and I feel guilty for not speaking when I have something to say. As I don't talk, I don't know that I have something to say. See how pretty it is?

— *I feel guilty toward Vladimir. I spoke to him yesterday, and I understood he is mirroring my own manifestation of spirituality. I saw how I try to impose on others how things should be. I thanked him for showing it to me. However, I did not see myself blaming him for not choosing his words more cautiously in order not to upset me. I see now that I blamed him.*

— *Can blame come without guilt?*

— No. It means you do not see the tail of the snake yet.

— *Is that so?*

— The tail is far away. The snake is long. It takes a long time for the head to reach the tail.

— *I blame myself for sensing with my body. I need to approach someone and touch him. I don't know why. I feel nervousness around my chest area. I don't know why. I suppress it.*

— It means, I blame myself for bodily manifestations and experience guilt in relationship with this.

— *I understand now.*

— *Can you help me to see my blame and guilt? I can mention a specific example, but as I understand it, this mechanism may work in other situations. Antony's manners irritate me. I cannot accept his mannerisms.*

— Which specific manner of his irritates you?

— *His laugh. His cell phone which is constantly ringing. His tone of voice.*

— Are you saying he is not serious enough?

— *On top of it, he is a womanizer. All of this leads to my blaming him.*

241

— You are blaming him for being a womanizer. That is one thing. You also blame him for not being serious. That is a totally different thing.

— *All of these things add up.*

— When you look at it this way, you can't see the parts that are being added. Let's take it apart. A lot of garbage was thrown into a trash can. I ask what exactly is there. I am being told, "Garbage." I take it apart, and I see many different things: pencils, pens, paper, old razors…

— *At this point, I am not sure what is in on top of my blame list.*

— Let's be very specific. What are you blaming him for? Are you blaming him for being a womanizer?

— *I am blaming him for his inability to pick up one woman and to stay with her.*

— *He is searching.*

— *How long can one search?*

— Okay. What did you have for breakfast?

— *I ate a bowl of cereal and a toast with butter. I also had a cup of tea.*

— Okay. So, you ate cereal, toast, butter, and you drunk a cup of tea. Why didn't you stop with one thing? Why didn't you just have a piece of bread?

— *I am not irritated by anyone. I like everyone here, and I accept them the way they are. I even started to accept Pint at one point.*

— "At one point and for a certain period of time." And what happened before, I don't remember, right?

— *Well, this is already in the past.*

— Continue.

— *I blame myself for not understanding anything. I blame myself for being an idiot. I blame myself for my being picked upon by you the second day in a row.*

— Do I pick on you? You are picking on yourself. That's what happens. If you say now that you blame yourself, you pick on yourself. Now you blame those that blame you, but you do it yourself. People just show it to you.

— *I can see that. I see people showing me my relationship to myself.*

— Yes. That is how you relate to yourself. So, what do you ask of those who show you how you relate to yourself?

— *I said it already. I blame myself. I feel guilty. I blame myself for being so stupid.*

— *Guilt for guilt.*

— Now, look at the blame you create and the guilt that happens to be the consequence of it. You feel and experience guilt for being told that you are stupid and do not understand anything. Your blame of others should be equal.

— *I, on the other hand, behave differently. I suppose this is not the case, and I blame those that talk about it.*

— You blame those who, according to you, say what they are not supposed to say. You tell them, "Get out of here. You do not understand anything yourself." You blame them, and as a result you get your guilt.

— *Yes, I do.*

The harder you blame, the guiltier you feel

— The more you blame others, the more guilt you will accumulate. You need to see that you manufacture this guilt yourself. In order to feel guilty, you have to blame. And the more you blame, the guiltier you will feel.

— *And I will continue to blame harder and harder.*

— Yes, blame escalates.

— *It seems to me that the goal of this seminar is for us to go home happy.*

243

— Hand in hand and singing nice songs, right?

— *And for her to leave happy too.*

— You don't say...

— *And then what are we?*

— *And how can you help her, Natasha?*

— *We should show her different points of view. Take a look at yourself from this point of view, and take a look at yourself from that point of view.*

— So, show her.

— *Everyone should try.*

— Why everyone? You wanted it. As they say, no good deed is going to go unpunished. You announced your desire to help her. So, help her. Do it.

— *I understand everyone is at his own level of consciousness, everyone sees the world his own way. Everyone's worldview is different.*

— You sang us a happy song and got pleasure out of it. When you say it, do it.

— *Then we all should feel guilty.*

— Don't bring others into it. You came up with this idea, and you should be the one to realize it. If you can't do it yourself, don't drag others into it. This was not their idea. It was your idea. I will tell you more. This is not even an idea. This is a delirious, happy song you sing to bring attention to yourself. You sang it. Now you are done. A little girl got on a chair, sang her song, and sat down. She is waiting for another opening to sing her song. However, you brought attention to yourself, and now I ask you to realize the words of your happy song.

— *Everyone here had probably thought about helping a crying woman, to come forward and to express pity. At the same time, you activate something, so one can experience it and get a boost of understanding. If I were to approach her on my own, I would take part of*

244

her guilt. If we all were to approach her, she would understand that we share her feeling of guilt and that we blame you.

— Exactly.

— I saw something opposite. I saw that I don't have any pity for Olga. I don't feel compassion towards her.

— **Compassion and pity are different things. Compassion occurs when you understand what happens to another human being because you know it inside yourself. Pity arises when you, not understanding what is going on in you, simply resonate to your own pity, projecting it onto someone else.**

— I experienced a feeling of guilt yesterday. A fellow human being felt bad, but I did not care. I immediately judged and blamed myself for this callous behavior.

— I blame myself for being unable to approach a fellow human being and to show attention to him. I blame myself for my inability to act on an impulse.

— We are moving from the feeling of pity to blame, when my question was why does a feeling of guilt appear?

— I am talking about guilt now.

— Then you should say, "I am not blaming. I feel guilty." Those are different things. Why do you feel guilty?

— I feel guilty because I am blaming.

— **I want to hear the specifics from you. You have to be very specific. Why do you feel guilty? Then, I will ask you, "How do you create this feeling of guilt?" and you will answer, "I blame."**

— I feel guilty because I blame another human being.

— This is the rule I brought to your attention. We need to get specifics and to use this rule in order to solve specific problems. There is a rule, and problems we address now should be solved by using this rule. **I defined the rule, and** now I invite you to solve some problems. These problems are solved the following way. You say, "I feel guilty for such and such things."

— *I did not start right.*

— You did not finish right either.

— *When I don't understand, I feel guilt that is equal in strength to my blame when I do not understand.*

— I asked you to talk about why exactly you feel guilty. Then you will find your blame.

— *Specifically, I blamed Olga just now.*

— I invited you to start with guilt. I feel guilty for …

— *Okay. I feel guilty when I say something here, and when I am shown that I do not understand something.*

— I feel guilty for…

— *I feel guilty for being stupid.*

— I feel guilty for not understanding.

— *Yes.*

— Now, what specific blame gave birth to this guilt.

— *The blame of not understanding.*

— I blame other people for their inability to understand. As a result, I feel guilty when I don't understand something myself. I receive what I send. So, the question is "How can I stop receiving what is unpleasant for me?" The answer is, "I have to stop sending what appears pleasant to me, but what also have an opposite side—what is unpleasant to me."

— *I feel very guilty when I feel I am insincere. I blame people heavily for insincerity. When this happens, it is very pleasant to feel how insincere he is and how sincere I am.*

A great method to see your dualities

— We are talking about a great method that allows you to connect your dualities. Who prevents you from applying it all the time? This method is simple. But in order to apply it, you need to feel guilty. **You carry guilt all the time, but you avoid feeling it. You keep blaming instead.**

— *There are only few instances when I remember feeling guilty. You are right; it is primarily blame that I feel.*

— And what do you do when you get together?

— *We blame others.*

— It seems to me that when I blame, I do not feel guilty. Therefore, I continue to blame.

— *I feel guilty for not saying everything I have to say, and I blame for the same reason.*

— *I feel guilty when I do something that I need to do, knowing that someone would be hurt by it. Then I start lying. I blame myself for lying. I blame myself for cheating.*

— I will ask you to continue this great conversation in pairs.

— *Can I ask everyone here to say out loud what irritates him or her in me?*

— *I am irritated by your disrespectful attitude toward women.*

— *I, on the other hand, feel I am missing something he has. I can't behave the way he does.*

— *Oleg feels women. A woman feels good being with him. You, on the other hand, are doing it with insulting superiority.*

— *In the beginning, I hated you. Now, I realize I am exactly like you.*

— What exactly is that?

— *Arrogance, disdain.*

— What else?

— *Disregard for women.*

— I am irritated by my seeing myself through him. His originality. People do a certain thing, but he does something else.

— He does something that is not accepted?

— His pose is irritating. It is a feminine pose.

— I am afraid of him. I am afraid of his jokes. They are unexpected.

— I am irritated by his interrogating stare.

— I am irritated that he does not know what he wants.

— Great. Don't forget you are talking about yourself. Do not waste the profit of awareness. Was your request satisfied? What affected you the most?

— Anna. She knows.

— Look how happy she is. Her blame hit the mark. What did you tell him? You told him he is not a man?

— Yes.

— But you are not a woman either. How do you feel?

— Bad. If one is to experience it fully, one feels very bad.

— I don't express myself here. I am not open. I have a sense of my exclusiveness. It seems to me that if I am to open up, my exclusiveness would disappear.

— You are unique now. You will be the same as everyone else.

— My uniqueness stimulates my arrogance and extravagant behavior. I don't like to talk the same way everybody else talks. From day one, I have had this inner desire to take part in unusual situations. It comes from my feeling of being exclusive.

— The exclusivity leads to exclusion. What about your relationship with women?

— I feel the same way with women, the same exclusivity.

— And what exactly constitutes your behavior?

— I get a woman interested in me, and then I run away.

— Why do you run away?

248

— I run away because otherwise everyone would see how common and plain I am. I would not be exclusive anymore.

Exclusivity excludes you

— What would happen if every tree on Earth were to think of its exclusivity? Trees will move ten miles away from each other. The ego thinks only about its exclusivity. But what is exclusivity? **Exclusivity is created by the exclusion of a certain side**. It is a tooth abscess. A specialist is like a tooth abscess. Its fullness is unilateral. But take a look at the abscess. Every genius here is a tooth abscess. The genius is being praised here because everyone wants to be exclusive in this reality. Exclusivity comes in combination with inner craziness and separation.

Everyone here tries to be original, suffers because of it, but does not want to abandon it. One needs to complete this circle. When you become aware and accept the oppositions of the ego, you turn into nobody and everything at the same time. You can become anything you want. You can turn into anyone or anything you want, not identifying with a chosen role. A good actor can play anything, and you will turn into a good actor.

A good actor easily takes a mask off and puts on another one. A good actor does not identify with a mask. Life is a theater. We are actors on stage. When you got to this theater, you developed into a certain personage, and the mask you picked up got glued to your face. It is still on you today. You are afraid of being nobody. You are afraid of losing yourself. But who are you? You are just a mask on a face of a personage you used to consider to be you. Is this personage really you?

When you release your illusory notions of yourself, you receive the universal key that will open every door of your house and allow you to experience any role without identifying with it. But as long as you identify with one role, you cannot play other roles. Someone tells you that you are not a man, and you get hysterical. But if you are Nobody and Everything, you can reply, "Yes, I am not a man. I am a woman." You are told, "You are not an adult," and you reply, "Yes, I know. I am a child." Do you feel all these roles in you?

— *I fight all my life. My life scenario is one of constant fight. I fight at work. I fight at home.*

— Why?

— *I fight to make my personality stronger.*

— I am not against you developing your personality. Moreover, the stage of development of your personality is a necessary stage. You need a developed personality to develop your essence. However, I work with people who are ready to become aware of and to transform their personalities. Until your personality is fully formed, you cannot transform it. **Until a cocoon is fully formed, a butterfly cannot emerge.** The school of holistic psychology is a place where caterpillars can metamorphose into butterflies.

There are plenty of schools, courses, and trainings geared to personal development, i.e. for caterpillars. Those schools are also necessary. The question is: "What do you need?"

— *I felt myself as a glass half filled with water floating in the ocean. The water in this glass spent its entire life trying to remain in this glass. It has used all its strength and all its power to not allow the ocean water to touch it. And now it has burst on its own, and it is in the ocean. During yesterday's dance exercise, I touched everyone. I tried to feel this new sensation of myself. I tried not to feel myself in a glass but to feel myself as "We." This was an amazing feeling. Then, I felt like dancing. I felt I was spinning a huge spiral freeing myself from something. Then everything ended. I started to breathe the way I did during the exercise. It was spontaneous. It was rhythmical. I suffer from severe arthritis that affects multiple joints. It is very painful. All my aches and pains are gone now.*

— I was amazed. You usually walk with a limp. And you were dancing like you were twenty years old.

— I have a feeling that I cannot describe yet, but it is very healthy.

— I saw the weakness I used to blame Antony for in myself. I felt this part of me. I felt the part of me that I did not allow to exist.

— Development of the intellect occurs through development of the emotional sphere. In order to move to a different quality of intellect, you need to use feelings.

— I saw uncertainty in myself. I want to do something, but then I become uncertain. It shakes me up. I make a step forward, and then I make two steps backwards.

— I saw myself blaming my own movements again. As soon as I get into this part and start to blame myself for certain physical movements, I become rigid and I can't move. I have a strong ban on manifesting my physical body.

— Some people in our group were dancing unnaturally. I told them to listen to their bodies. We had a very interesting experience. It was obvious that body movements were under the brain's control. We could not do anything about it. So, I spent some time looking outside. I observed the wind that was blowing. I observed the trees moving. I saw the spontaneity of it. I felt it, and something changed.

— This was not a usual dance. A usual dance represents a number of learned movements. You have to allow your body to manifest itself.

— When you let go of everything, certain movements come through you that you do not know or understand. Your body has a life of its own.

— Yes.

— During my conversation with Lillian, I recalled how cruel I was to my sister and to other women. I also recalled different manifestations of sexual cruelty. Three students discussed their past depressions and suicidal ideations. Suddenly, it dawned on me that I also tried to commit suicide before.

— We live in hell. Sometimes you start to think that you need to self-liquidate. However, you entered this world with a task that you need to accomplish. To self-liquidate is to refuse to accomplish this task.

— I was born in Uzbekistan. I recalled that my mother said I could have been brought up Uzbek. When I was born, a mistake occurred in the hospital. Another baby was brought to my mother to be fed. I was given to an Uzbek woman. My mother's maternal instinct did not turn on, but the Uzbek woman ran into the room, threw me on my mother's bed, and took her baby. I am being shown again and again that our souls plan definitive scenarios for each one of us to acquire a certain, specific experience.

— I want to thank people that came for the first time. I want to thank all our parts. I feel that these people attended our seminars before. I feel warmth and acceptance coming from them. Seeing them getting into difficult situations and their reaction to these situations, I understand that this is not the reaction of the novices who came for the first time. I see the good will with which they take criticism. I see their intention to get out of what they got stuck in. I am grateful to them.

— I want to express my gratitude. I am here for the first time. I have never looked at life from the point of view of duality. What I saw here opens my worldview and allows me to look at my life from many different sides. There is a lot of work ahead.

— Yes. But now you don't need to wander in search of the unknown. There is specific work ahead of you.

— During this seminar, I saw how deep my sleep is.

—That is awareness. Awareness allows you to see the depth of your sleep. The more aware you are, the more you can see the depth of your sleep. This is a paradox. I see how deep my sleep is, but at the same time, I am aware of it.

www.ingramcontent.com/pod-product-compliance
Lightning Source LLC
Chambersburg PA
CBHW062049270326
41931CB00013B/3007